FAMOUS FIRST FLIGHTS
ACROSS THE ATLANTIC

FAMOUS FIRST FLIGHTS

ACROSS THE ATLANTIC

Frank J. Delear

ILLUSTRATED WITH PHOTOGRAPHS

DODD, MEAD & COMPANY, NEW YORK

1 2 3 4 5 6 7 8 9 10

Library of Congress Cataloging in Publication Data

Delear, Frank J
    Famous first flights across the Atlantic.

    Bibliography: p.
    Includes index.
    SUMMARY: Includes, among others, such historical
flights across the Atlantic as the very first flight,
the first non-stop flight, and the first mass crossing.
    1. Transatlantic flights—Juvenile literature.
[1. Transatlantic flights] I. Title.
TL531.D34   629.13′091′1   79-12808
ISBN 0-396-07704-8

To Marion,
for her love and encouragement, and to our five favorite people:
Susan, David, Betsy, James, and *Janet*

"We have all known flights when of a sudden . . . there has come a premonition of an incursion into a forbidden world whence it was going to be infinitely difficult to return. Thus, when Mermoz first crossed the South Atlantic in a hydroplane, as day was dying he ran foul of the Black Hole region, off Africa. Straight ahead of him were the tails of tornadoes rising minute by minute gradually higher, rising as a wall is built; and then the night came down upon these preliminaries and swallowed them up; and when, an hour later, he slipped under the clouds, he came out into a fantastic kingdom.

"Great black waterspouts had reared themselves seemingly in the immobility of temple pillars. Swollen at their tops, they were supporting the squat and lowering arch of the tempest, but through the rifts in the arch there fell slabs of light and the full moon sent her radiant beams between the pillars down upon the frozen tiles of the sea. Through these uninhabited ruins Mermoz made his way, gliding slantwise from one channel of light to the next, circling round those giant pillars in which there must have rumbled the upsurge of the sea, flying for four hours through these corridors of moonlight toward the exit from the temple. And this spectacle was so overwhelming that only after he had got through the Black Hole did Mermoz awaken to the fact that he had not been afraid."

—from *Wind, Sand and Stars*
by Antoine de Saint-Exupery

ACKNOWLEDGMENTS

For his kind response to my calls for help, and for his various suggestions and information, I express grateful appreciation to my good friend Harvey H. Lippincott, United Technologies archivist and a most knowledgeable aviation historian. Special thanks also to John W. R. Taylor, editor, *Jane's All the World's Aircraft*, a prolific and authoritative aviation writer whose worldwide renown needs no further embellishment from me, and to Robert O. Anthony, advisor to Walter Lippmann Papers, Yale University, who took time out from a demanding work schedule to provide a variety of source material.

My sincere thanks also to Gordon Nelson of Squantum, Massachusetts, a friend and early aviation enthusiast; Lord Ventry, authority on British airship history; David R. Smith, Airship International Press; William K. Kaiser and Richard A. Winsche, Nassau (New York) County Museum; R. F. (Bill) Bailey, British Aerospace Dynamics Group; Norman Barfield, Vickers Ltd.; John A. Bagley, Science Museum, London; Richard C. Holmquist, Jr., United Technologies, Paris; Dan DeVito and Donald G. Fertman, Sikorsky Aircraft; Ralph B. Lightfoot, retired engineering manager, Sikorsky Aircraft; Daniel Z. Henkin, Air Transport Association; Robert I. Stanfield, aviation editor and writer; James E. Burke, U.S. Naval Institute Proceedings; Anna McManus Larson, *Yankee* Magazine; Anne Morrow Lindbergh; Judith A. Schiff, chief manuscript archivist, Yale Library; Beatrice LaFlamme, United Technologies archives; Patty Maddox, U.S. Naval Institute; Royal D. Frey, The Air Force Museum; Giorgio Apostolo, aviation historian, Milan, Italy; Major Eric Anderson, U.S. Air Force pictorial branch; Erich W. Mueller, Russelsheim, Germany; Jean Ross Howard, Aerospace Industries Association; Dominick A. Pisano, reference librarian, National Air and Space Museum, Smithsonian Institution; Lewis R. Berlepsch, aviation historian; Ben L. Abruzzo, balloonist, *Double Eagle II*; and Lieutenant Commander Denis W. Delear, Louis A. Barrett, Russell C. Estey, and Russell V. Booth, for research assistance.

CONTENTS

FAMOUS FIRST FLIGHTS
ACROSS THE ATLANTIC

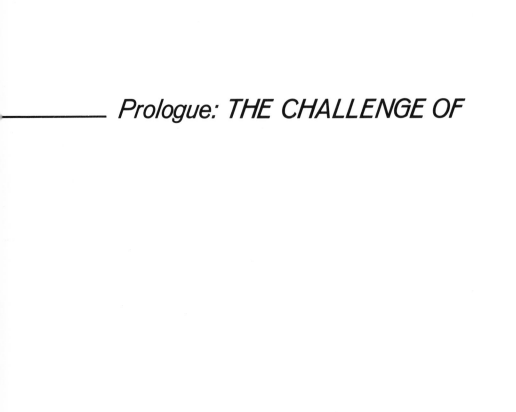

Prologue: THE CHALLENGE OF

THE ATLANTIC _____

WHY DID so many men—and women—attempt to fly the Atlantic during the 1920s and early 1930s? What moved them to take off in overloaded aircraft of wood and fabric with little more than a compass and a prayer, knowing that others before them had perished? Fame, money, or some nobler purpose—what drove them to risk their lives on the beat of a single engine and the hope that fair skies and favorable winds would see them safely across?

Writing in 1937 after the disappearance of Amelia Earhart in the Pacific, the late Walter Lippmann provides at least part of the answer. In words which apply to all adventurous spirits, before and since, he wrote:

"The world is a better place to live in because it contains human beings who will give up ease and security and stake their own lives in order to do what they themselves think worth doing. . . . The best things of mankind are as useless as Amelia Earhart's adventure. They are the things undertaken not for some definite, measurable result, but because someone, not counting the costs or calculating the consequences, is moved by curiosity, the love of excellence, a point of honor, the compulsion to invent or to make or to understand. In such persons mankind overcomes the inertia which would keep it earthbound forever in its habitual ways. They have in them the free and useless energy with which alone men surpass themselves."

Such people, Lippmann continued, "have been possessed for a time with an extraordinary passion which is unintelligible in ordinary terms. No preconceived theory fits them. No material purpose actuates them. They do the useless, brave, noble, the divinely foolish, and the very wisest things that are done by man. And what they prove to themselves and to others is that man is no mere creature of his habits, no mere automaton in his routine, no mere cog in the collective machine, but that in the dust of which he is made there is also fire, lighted now and then by great winds from the sky."

In her own way Amelia Earhart expressed the same thoughts. She said that she flew the Atlantic twice because she *wanted to*, which drew criticism as being a foolhardy reason. But her critics overlooked her following words: "It isn't, I think, a reason to be apologized for by man or woman. It is the most honest motive for the majority of mankind's achievements. To want in one's own heart to do a thing for its own sake; to enjoy doing it; to concentrate all one's energies upon it—that is not only the surest guarantee of its success, it is also being true to oneself."

Such are the kind of people we shall be talking about in the pages ahead. These, of course, were the successful ones, the survivors, who made it across, achieving the "famous firsts." Still there were others, most of them all but forgotten, who did not survive, some because they were not properly prepared: Clavier and Islamoff; Davis and Wooster; Nungesser and Coli; Bertaud, Payne, and Hill; Tully and Medcalf; Omdahl, Goldsborough, Schroeder, and Mrs. Grayson; Hinchcliffe and Miss Mackay; MacLaren and Mrs. Hart; and others over other oceans as well as the Atlantic. There were some, also, who succeeded, only to be lost on later flights, most notably the great French aviator, Jean Mermoz, who made four pioneering air mail flights across the South Atlantic in 1930 and 1933 before disappearing on a fifth flight in 1936.

Speaking at the Paris Air Museum, Le Bourget Field, in June, 1977, fifty years after her famous husband's epic flight, Anne Morrow Lindbergh paid tribute to those who lost their lives:

"Today we are celebrating not only my husband's flight, but a whole era of gallant aviators and their flights. Though these fliers came from different nations, they were in a sense brothers with a common aim: to prove by their long-distance flights and record-breaking hops that aviation could increase communication, commerce, and understanding between people. . . .

"But in celebrating the successes we should not forget the attempts that did not succeed. *It took just as much courage to attempt and fail as it did to attempt and succeed.*"

(Excerpts from Mr. Lippmann, courtesy of the Robert O. Anthony Collection of Walter Lippmann. Excerpts from Anne Morrow Lindbergh, courtesy of Mrs. Lindbergh.)

1 COMMANDER READ AND

THE NC-4

First Across _____

ONE OF FLYING'S more frightening experiences is the "near miss," the accidental passing of two aircraft dangerously close to each other while in flight.

On the night of May 16, 1919, one of history's outstanding transatlantic flights came within a few feet and a few seconds of disaster when not two, but three aircraft experienced a near miss 4,000 feet above the mid-Atlantic. The aircraft were the U.S. Navy's giant flying boats, the NC-1, NC-3, and NC-4.

At the time the lumbering, four-engined biplanes were cruising at their normal 75 to 80 miles an hour and were over 300 miles along on their attempt to make the first crossing of the Atlantic by air.

The NC-4 on a test flight before its historic transatlantic flight.

A little luck, a moonlit night, and some quick, evasive action combined to avert what almost certainly would have been a fatal collision. With the moment of danger passed, the flight pressed on through the night, eventually to bring aviation immortality to one of the three planes.

In retrospect that close call above the ocean seems typical of the troubles which plagued not only the flight but the long months of preparation leading up to it. Despite difficulties, though, the imagination, courage, and determination of a small group of Naval aviators kept the daring project alive even when, at times, it seemed that all was lost.

The story of the NC boats had its beginning in 1917, more than a year before the end of World War I. German U-boats were sinking a great many Allied vessels, including some in which airplanes were being shipped overseas to be used in bombing the undersea craft. The Navy decided the situation required aircraft large enough to fly across the Atlantic.

In September, 1917, the Navy commissioned Glenn Curtiss, a pioneer pilot and seaplane builder, to design a flying boat able to carry sufficient bombs, depth charges, and guns to destroy enemy submarines. The order was for four such ships to be built at the Curtiss plant at Garden City on Long Island in New York. A giant hangar was erected, meanwhile, at the Naval Air Station at nearby Rockaway Beach to house two of the huge aircraft. The new flying boats were designated NC (for Navy/Curtiss) and were soon nicknamed "Nancies." Spearheading the project were Admiral Douglas W. Taylor, chief of the Navy's Construction Corps; and Commanders Holden C. Richardson (who de-

Commander Holden C. Richardson, NC-3 pilot, designed the huge hulls of the NC flying boats.

U.S. NAVY

signed the hulls), G. C. Westervelt, and J. C. Hunsaker.

The idea of crossing the Atlantic by air had tempted men from the earliest days of flying. Balloons and nonrigid airships had made a few unsuccessful attempts. In 1913 Lord North-cliffe, a leading British newspaper publisher, offered a $50,000 award for the first transatlantic flight between the United States, Canada, or Newfoundland and Ireland or England (in either direction) in 72 hours. Landings on the water for repairs, and even towing, were permitted. The war delayed the race for over four years, but by the spring of 1919 three British planes were in Newfoundland being prepared for the risky flight, while a fourth was en route by sea to join the competition.

The NC-1 made its first flight October 4, 1918, at Rockaway Beach with Commander Richardson at the controls and a crew of five aboard. The craft, the world's largest flying boat, made an impressive sight with its squat, gray hull and bright, yellow wings spanning an unprecedented 126 feet. Mounted high on

Mechanics clean and over-haul the NC-4's Liberty en-gines in preparation for the transatlantic flight.

U.S. NAVY

wooden booms was a boxlike tail assembly twice the size of the standard fighter planes of the day. The NC-1 flew very well. On November 25, 1918, its three 400-horsepower Liberty engines straining to their utmost, the NC-1 flew with 51 men aboard, a world record at the time.

With the end of World War I, the NC boats' original purpose —submarine hunting—no longer existed. The project was in danger of being abandoned when a new goal appeared: why not use the NC boats to make the first air crossing of the Atlantic? Such a flight would help strengthen Naval aviation and make a major contribution to air progress in general.

Ignoring some complaints of "publicity stunt," the Navy approved a plan to fly the Nancies from Trepassey Bay, Newfoundland, to the Azores, a 1,300-mile over-water hop, and then on to Portugal and England. The plan included spotting destroyers and battleships at 50-mile intervals along the route as a safety measure. The vessels would also fire star shells to help

The NC-4 on seaplane ramp at Naval Air Station, Rockaway Beach, Long Island.

keep the fliers on course. May 16 was chosen as the date because there would be a full moon, a night flight being selected so the planes could land in daylight at the Azores. The Navy was not seeking Lord Northcliffe's $50,000 prize. Anyway, the rules had been changed and now called for a nonstop flight with no water landings permitted.

Work was speeded up on the NC program, with subcontractor companies in Massachusetts, Rhode Island, and New York building the remaining hulls, wings, and tail sections. Using the lessons learned with the NC-1, Navy and Curtiss engineers made many design changes. They added a fourth engine behind the center engine, so that the three original power plants pulled and the fourth pushed the planes through the air. They moved the pilot's cockpit from the center engine nacelle down and forward to the front of the hull.

The program was moving along well when the first trouble struck. A March storm battered the NC-1 onto the beach, damaging the hull and a wing. The ship was repaired with parts from the NC-2 (which had not been flying very well) and the planned four-plane flight was reduced to three. On May 5 both the NC-1 and NC-4 were damaged in a hangar fire, but were returned to service with parts again cannibalized from the NC-2. On the next day a crowd waiting to see the NC boats take off for Halifax, Nova Scotia, watched in horror as a small seaplane crashed into a fuel storage tank, killing the two-man crew. The takeoff was delayed until May 7, but the troubles continued: shortly before departure a mechanic lost his hand when he stepped too close to a whirling propeller of the NC-4.

Despite these ill omens, the flight took off at 10:00 A.M. on May 7. In charge was Commander John H. Towers, a pioneer Naval aviator, who headed the newly formed NC Seaplane Division 1. Towers' flagship was the NC-3, piloted by Commander Richardson. The NC-1 was skippered by Lieutenant Commander Patrick Bellinger with Lieutenant Commander Marc A. Mitscher as pilot. Lieutenant Commander Albert C. Read, a

Lieutenant Commander Albert C. Read, in charge of the NC-4.

U.S. NAVY

diminutive (5-4, 120 pounds) and quiet-spoken Vermont native, commanded the NC-4 with First Lieutenant Elmer F. Stone of the U.S. Coast Guard as pilot. Each plane carried a crew of six—the commander, pilot, copilot, pilot-engineer, radio operator, and engineer.

Trouble struck at 2:00 P.M. on the flight to Nova Scotia. The NC-4, fast becoming a jinx plane, landed at sea when first one and then a second engine failed. The other planes flew on and reached Halifax at 7:00 P.M. The next day they bounced and shuddered through stormy weather to Trepassey Bay.

The NC-4, riding the ocean swells 80 miles northeast of the Naval Air Station at Chatham, on Cape Cod, taxied all night on its remaining two engines, reaching Chatham at dawn. Repairs were made and, on May 13, the NC-4 was off again for Halifax,

Close-up view shows the NC-4's engines and wooden propellers.

U.S. NAVY

The NC-4 60 miles at sea en route to Halifax, Nova Scotia, first leg of its transatlantic trip. Photo taken from Navy scout escort.

reaching that city despite the rough running of three engines. After more engine repairs the jinx ship took off for Newfoundland the morning of May 15. Within minutes, Read and his men were again on the water, as usual with a faulty engine. The problem, a plugged fuel line, was quickly fixed and the NC-4 lifted from the sea at noon.

Descending for their landing at Trepassey Bay, the crew of the NC-4 met an unpleasant surprise: the NC-1 and NC-3 were speeding through the water on their takeoff runs. Towers had decided to leave for the Azores without the tardy and troublesome NC-4. Then fate stepped in to change aviation history. The two flying boats, overloaded and running in a crosswind, were unable to get airborne. The NC-4 landed, the other ships returned to base, and the flight was rescheduled for the next day. Inaccurate fuel gauges, it was found, had caused the NC-1 and NC-3 to be overloaded with gasoline.

Read ordered a new engine and three new propellers installed on the NC-4. The ship was poised for the real flight now and he was determined to erase its jinx label once and for all.

Trepassey Bay resounded to the drone of twelve Liberty engines as the three flying boats taxied out and began their takeoff runs on the afternoon of May 16. The NC-4, with 70 pounds of oil tossed overboard to lighten the load, became airborne, but the others remained stuck on the water. Even with the proper fuel load they were still too heavy. Aboard the NC-3, Towers threw out one of his two radios, a bag of "first cover" mail and put ashore one of his two engineers. The NC-1 was also lightened. Read, circling overhead, finally landed to await the others. Then all three took off, the NC-4 again climbing much faster.

The three planes were supposed to fly in formation, but several factors interfered with that plan. First, the NC-4 proved faster and kept pulling ahead of the others. Second, the NC-3's wiring had been soaked during the takeoff run, blacking out both its wingtip and cockpit lights. Third, the darkness and a cloud overcast made close formation flying difficult and dangerous. In addition, the question of whether the planes or the Navy vessels on the sea were exactly on course became uncertain as the flight progressed. Soon the planes were "on their own." Eventually, all these factors led to the near disaster mentioned earlier.

Looking down, Towers in the NC-3 suddenly saw the NC-4 directly below and very close. At almost the same moment, Read glanced up, sighted the NC-3 and quickly veered the NC-4 off and down. Only the moonlight, silhouetting the blacked-out NC-3, had enabled Read to see the other ship while there was still time to avoid a collision.

Seconds later, Towers caught a glimpse of the NC-1 passing above only a scant 50 feet overhead. Bellinger, in the NC-1, had not even seen the darkened NC-3!

Again the NC-4 pulled ahead, with engines, instruments, and

navigation almost perfect. Then rain, fog, and rough air brought problems. The stars became obscured, while the star shells and searchlights of the surface ships were no longer visible. The turbulence increased and the crews, tossed roughly about, became unsure as to exactly where they were. They dropped lower through the fog, probing for a glimpse of the sea. The NC-4 fell into a spin, broke through beneath the clouds and recovered, barely missing a crash into the water.

Read, whose specialty was navigation, finally determined his position and continued with confidence toward the Azores. The skies cleared for a while but soon became foggy again. Read began to worry about the Azores' high mountains, hidden somewhere ahead in the fog. Suddenly, through a break in the clouds he spotted Flores, one of the western islands of the Azores. The flight's planned destination, Ponta Delgada, still lay over 200 miles away. More bad weather prompted Read to set the NC-4 down in the harbor at Horta. They had been airborne for 15 hours, 18 minutes and, thanks to the usual west-to-east tailwind, had achieved an average surface speed of 94 miles an hour.

Meanwhile, the NC-3, flying blind through thick fog, had only two hours of fuel left. Towers, though off course, guessed he must be nearing the Azores and he, like Read, also began to worry about hitting one of the islands' towering peaks. He decided to land on the sea and wait for clearer weather. As the NC-3 broke through the clouds, the crew thought the sea looked fairly smooth. But ocean swells are deceptive. The aircraft struck a swell, several engine struts failed, and the frames of the hull were split. No one was injured and the rugged hull still floated, but further flying was impossible.

Bellinger, farther north, faced the same fog problem and also decided to land—with even worse results. As the NC-1 touched down, a huge wave tore off its lower tail section. Both flying boats now lay dead in the water and, since they were off course, were far removed from the surface ships which had begun a search. The NC-1 was some 100 miles from Flores and the NC-3 about 50 miles closer to that island. Both were over 200 miles short of their planned destination, Ponta Delgada on the island of São Miguel.

Though badly damaged, the NC-1 was able to limp through the rough seas for five hours before being spotted by a Greek ship, the *Ionia*, which took the six seasick fliers aboard. Later, when the destroyer *Gridley* arrived, Bellinger and his crew were transferred to the American vessel. The *Gridley* took the NC-1 in tow, but this brought more damage to the aircraft. The destroyer then rammed and sank the flying boat to prevent it from becoming a menace to shipping.

Many miles from the searching ships, Towers and his men fought to keep the NC-3 afloat. The waves washed the left wing float away and the men took turns perched far out on the right wing to keep the ship from capsizing. They drifted eastward through the night of May 17 and at dawn could see the peaks of mountains in the distance. Pilot Richardson held the NC-3

The NC-4 sets down in the Tagus River off Lisbon, Portugal, at the end of its epic crossing of the Atlantic.

U.S. NAVY

The NC-4 enters the harbor at Lisbon, after completing the first crossing of the Atlantic by air.

headed into the wind and the ship continued its sternward drift to the east. This drift, plus Towers' skilled use of a sea anchor and one engine, finally brought the crippled NC-3 into the harbor at Ponta Delgada the morning of May 19. There the gallant craft received a roaring welcome from ships' whistles and even a 21-gun salute.

The battered NC-3 never flew again. Yet its journey was a victory of sorts—a 1,200-mile flight followed by over 60 hours of tossing through stormy seas to become the first of the three Nancies to reach the first stop they had planned when they took off from Newfoundland.

After being weathered in at Horta for days, Read and the NC-4 reached Ponta Delgada the following day (May 20) after a short hop of 1 hour, 45 minutes. One week later (May 27) they landed in the harbor at Lisbon, Portugal, 9 hours, 43 minutes out of the Azores, the first airplane ever to fly the Atlantic. In nineteen days (41 hours and 51 minutes in the air) they had traveled 3,322 miles. On May 31 the NC-4 ended its journey, landing at Plymouth, England, after a flight through rain and fog across the Bay of Biscay and the English Channel. Her crew, besides Read and pilot Stone, included Lieutenant Walter Hinton, copilot; Lieutenant James L. Breese, pilot-engineer; Ensign Herbert C. Rodd, radio operator; and Chief Machinist Mate Eugene S. Rhoads, engineer.

What of the other fliers, poised in Newfoundland and preparing to risk their lives for the $50,000 *Daily Mail* prize? First to leave (on May 18) were Harry Hawker, a colorful test pilot, and Kenneth Mackenzie-Grieve, navigator, in the single-engined

Following its transatlantic flight, the NC-4 was displayed in New York's Central Park to aid Navy recruitment.

U.S. NAVY

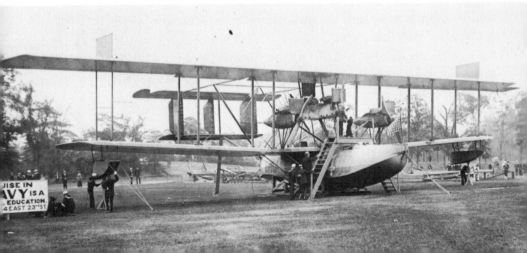

With its 126-foot wingspread, the NC-4 dominates the Naval Air Museum at Pensacola, Florida, final home of the history-making flying boat.

Sopwith biplane, the *Atlantic*. An overheated engine forced them to ditch in the sea alongside the Danish vessel, *Mary*, over 1,000 miles east of Newfoundland. The *Mary* had no radio and it was a week before she reached Scotland with the miraculous news that Hawker and Mackenzie-Grieve, all but given up for dead, had survived.

F. P. Raynham, pilot, and C.W.F. Morgan in the single-engined Martinsyde biplane, *Raymor*, crashed on takeoff (also on May 18), seriously injuring Morgan. Waiting to take off was a Handley Page V/1500, a huge World War I bomber with four engines and a wingspan of 126 feet, which carried a crew of four. Also awaiting takeoff was a fourth competitor, a twin-engined Vickers Vimy World War I bomber. Preparing the Vimy for the hazardous hop eastward were Captain John Alcock, pilot, and Lieutenant Arthur Whitten Brown, navigator—which brings us to our next Atlantic first.

2 ALCOCK, BROWN, AND

THE VIMY
First Nonstop ⸺⸺⸺⸺⸺

ON A SNOWY, rainy day in France in November, 1915, an un-armed British reconnaissance plane, riddled with machine gun slugs from German fighters, crash-landed behind the enemy lines. The pilot escaped unhurt, but the observer suffered an injury to his left leg which was to leave him with a limp for the rest of his life. The injured man, Arthur Whitten (Ted) Brown, a serious-minded young second lieutenant in the Royal Flying Corps when he was shot down, spent the following two years as a prisoner of war. This gave him ample time for serious thinking, a situation which eventually changed the course of his life.

Less than two years later, on the night of September 30, 1917, a big, twin-engined Handley Page 0/400 bomber of Britain's

Royal Naval Air Service, its port propeller shattered by Turkish antiaircraft fire, ditched at sea in the Gulf of Saros, a half mile off the enemy coast. The pilot, Flight Lieutenant John Alcock, and two crewmen swam ashore but were captured the next day and spent the rest of the war in a succession of Turkish prison camps. During his captivity, Alcock, though fun-loving and flamboyant, still found time (like Brown) for some serious thinking about his future.

Fate contrived in 1919 to bring the two men together and later to link forever the names Alcock and Brown as aviation immortals. Two more different personalities could hardly have been found. Alcock, stocky and clad usually in rumpled tweeds, was full of laughter and practical jokes. Six years younger than Brown, he was serious about only one subject—aviation. Learning to fly in 1912, at age twenty, he had quickly become a skilled pilot. He worked and flew with the great airmen of the day, including the British pilot-designers A.V. Roe and T.O.M. Sopwith.

Brown, a shy and studious man, dressed with military neatness and precision. He was born in England of American parents. (His father had helped plan and build a new Westinghouse Company factory in Manchester, England.) Brought up in a household devoted to education and engineering, young Brown also worked for Westinghouse and spent two years in South Africa as a mechanical engineer before World War I. Returning to England, he joined the RFC and soon developed a keen interest in aerial navigation.

While prisoners of war, both Alcock and Brown dreamed of flying the Atlantic some day, as pilot and navigator, respectively. That dream was about all they had in common, with one exception—their great respect for each other. But that goal was all that was needed to open the door to one of the greatest of all aviation achievements.

Toward the end of the first World War, Lord Northcliffe reinstated the *Daily Mail*'s offer of $50,000 for the first nonstop transatlantic flight. The prize was revived, the newspaper said, "to stimulate the production of more powerful engines and more suitable aircraft." The airplane builders quickly voiced their optimism. "A flight of 1,880 miles is no problem with existing machines," said Sopwith. Especially confident were Vickers Aviation, with its twin-engined Vimy, and Handley Page with its new four-engined V/1500. Several single-engined planes also appeared to have sufficient range for a nonstop crossing. By early 1919 there were eleven contenders—nine from Great Britain and one each from Italy and the United States. The latter, a twin-engined seaplane, the *Sunrise*, crashed during a test flight in March, 1919. Of the eleven, only four reached Newfoundland, the jumping-off place for the west-to-east crossing.

Alcock, still dreaming of a transatlantic flight, went to the Vickers company in March, 1919, at a time when Vickers still had not filed an official entry for the *Daily Mail* prize. Through sheer enthusiasm, the young pilot talked the company into

John Alcock, left, and Arthur Whitten Brown after arrival in Newfoundland to prepare for their transatlantic flight.

VICKERS LTD.

building a modified Vimy bomber for the transatlantic attempt. The Vimy, with two 360-horsepower Rolls Royce Eagle engines, each driving a four-bladed wooden propeller, cruised at 90 miles an hour and had a range of 2,440 miles. The modified craft could carry 865 gallons of gasoline, thanks to extra fuel tanks housed in the bomb compartments. For better communication, the pilot and navigator sat side by side in an open cockpit in the Vimy's nose, a change from the original arrangement of two single cockpits in tandem.

Vickers had been unable to find a good navigator for the ocean flight and Alcock, though preferring the additional help, was willing to risk flying alone. Luckily, in late March, Brown visited Vickers looking for a job. With his shy manner he was not impressive—until he mentioned his skill as a navigator. Questions followed and Brown described in detail his ideas for long-distance air navigation and how he'd planned a transatlantic flight route while a prisoner of war. Vickers officials knew they had found their navigator. Brown was introduced to Alcock, given a look at the nearly completed Vimy, and was promptly hired.

From the start, the contrast between the two men was clear: Alcock that day wore overalls and a gaudy tweed jacket, while Brown appeared natty in his RFC uniform set off by tie, gloves, and walking stick. Within minutes the two opposites were deep in a discussion of the proposed flight, even plotting a course in chalk on the hangar floor. Soon they felt the glow of a new friendship.

An almost impossible task faced Alcock, Brown, and the Vickers company. In the shortest possible time they had to complete the Vimy, test fly it, and ship it, dismantled, to Newfoundland— all in the faint hope that they would be in time to compete. Their competitors, meanwhile, were already in Newfoundland clearing airfields and preparing their planes for takeoff about April 16, the night of the next full moon.

Bad weather and soggy airfields in Newfoundland, as well as continuing storms over the Atlantic, prevented the Sopwith *Atlantic* and Martinsyde *Raymor* starting their ocean flights in mid-April and kept them earthbound for many days afterward. Encouraged by this news, Alcock took the Vimy up on its first flight on April 18 at the Vickers plant in Weybridge, England. The Vimy flew well and over the next few days Alcock and Brown made several more flights, including one of ten hours. They paid special attention to the engines, the navigational instruments (selected by Brown), and their new electrically heated flying suits. With everything functioning adequately, the Vimy was dismantled for shipment. Alcock, Brown, and four technicians left England for Halifax, Nova Scotia, on May 4 on the liner *Mauretania*. The crated Vimy, with seven more team members, left later on the freighter *Glendevon*. The advance party would have about two weeks to complete preparations while awaiting arrival of the Vimy on the slow freighter.

Traveling by local boat and train from Halifax, Alcock and Brown reached St. John's, Newfoundland, on May 13. There they found nothing but problems, chiefly the cold, wet, windy weather and the lack of a suitable airfield. Hawker and Mackenzie-Grieve with the *Atlantic* were using a patch of land at Glendenning's farm, six miles outside the city; Morgan and Raynham with the *Raymor* had leased some cleared land at nearby Quidi Vidi Lake, while the Handley Page group was camped on a strip of pasture at Harbour Grace, 60 miles from St. John's. There seemed to be nothing else left. Day after day Alcock and Brown left their rooms at St. John's Cochrane Hotel, bouncing over country roads in a borrowed Buick as they looked in vain for a suitable airfield.

Shortly before 4:00 P.M. on May 18, the *Atlantic* finally got away, staggering into the air from the rough gound of Glendenning's farm and heading out over the ocean. Hawker and Mackenzie-Grieve flew for 15 hours, mostly in stormy weather, covering 1,400 miles before an overheated engine forced them into the sea. Luckily the winds had carried them 150 miles south of their course and into the shipping lanes. As noted earlier, they were picked up by the Danish ship *Mary*, reaching Scotland five days later. Miraculously alive, they were hailed as heroes in England despite the failure of their flight. Hawker later won fame as the builder of warplanes in World War II, notably the Hawker Hurricane fighter.

An hour after the *Atlantic*'s departure on May 18, Morgan and Raynham began their takeoff run in the *Raymor* at Quidi Vidi. The takeoff, crosswind, proved more than the heavily loaded little plane could handle. It lifted into the air after 600 feet, but a wing dipped and the *Raymor* plowed into the ground, crashing its nose and forward section. Surprisingly, there was no fire and both men climbed from the wreck, Raynham with only minor cuts but Morgan with slivers of compass glass in his skull, injuries which cost him an eye.

Two up and two down; it had been a bad day for British aviation. At Harbour Grace, things were not much better, for the big Handley Page was experiencing many mechanical problems and seemed at least two weeks away from a takeoff. Suddenly the Vimy, the dark horse of the race, became the favorite.

The crated Vimy, arriving at St. John's on May 26, was trucked to Quidi Vidi where Raynham had loaned his field (at no charge) for assembly and test flights, now that he was out of the race. It was a temporary site, since the field did not provide the 1,500-foot run needed for takeoff of a fully loaded Vimy. Working twelve to fourteen hours a day, the crew assembled the big biplane in the open, despite cold, rain, and wind.

June brought better weather and the long-sought larger field. The trucker, a Mr. Lester, offered Alcock a meadow at his farm near Munday's Pond, on the outskirts of St. John's. There was one "catch": the ground had to be levelled, cleared of boulders, a stone wall, and some trees, and a drainage ditch filled in.

Partially assembled Vimy is pushed to final assembly area at Quidi Vidi Lake near St. John's, Newfoundland.

Three days of hard work by Lester's men, the Vickers team, and local volunteers resulted in a cleared strip some 1,200 feet long —not enough, but with wind and a little luck, it might suffice.

On June 9 the Vimy made its first flight in Newfoundland. Lightly loaded, the ship lifted from the Quidi Vidi strip in only

Crew places Vimy's upper left wing in position as the aircraft's assembly nears completion at Quidi Vidi in May, 1919.

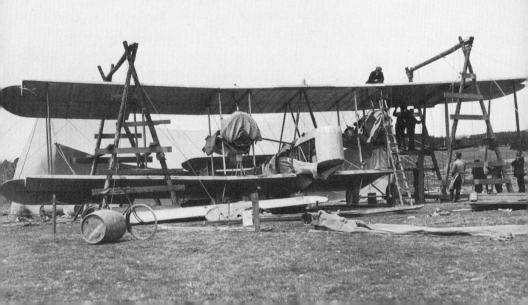

Townspeople from St. John's were regular visitors as the Vimy was readied for flight.

600 feet, circled over St. John's, swung briefly out over the ocean and then inland to the new field at Lester's farm. There Alcock made a perfect three-point landing, but had to turn in a sweeping "ground loop" to avoid a stone wall at the end of the field.

Alcock and Brown were ready to go, but then came a series of setbacks. The radio, for some reason, had failed in flight and had to be removed for tear-down and inspection. Winds of near gale force swept the area for two days without letup, endangering the tied-down Vimy. Fuel reserves, shipped from England in steel drums, were contaminated by a rubber lining in the drums. (Raynham gave Vickers his reserves.) As a final frustration, Vickers officials in England, enjoying fine spring weather, wired a tactless, "Please cable reason for non-start"!

A broken shock absorber on the Vimy's landing gear prevented start of the Atlantic flight on Friday, May 13. Supersti-
tion aside, it was just as well, in view of the rain and gale winds
prevailing. The weather improved the next day, with clear skies
and tailwinds predicted all the way to Ireland. The winds were
still too gusty, though, for a takeoff.

By noon the wind blew from the west, straight down the airstrip, which ran uphill from east to west. That meant an uphill
takeoff, since a downwind attempt (even with the added speed
of a downhill run) would be too risky for the fully loaded Vimy
on such a short field.

Spectators arrived, for it was Saturday and the factory work-
ers and storekeepers of St. John's had the afternoon off. Some set
up family picnics and others helped push the Vimy into position.
By one o'clock the wind had dropped to a steady 30 miles an
hour and, with a takeoff near, the field was cleared of horses and
sheep. Sandwiches, coffee, chocolate, a bottle of whiskey, and a

*Clad in heavy flying suits,
Alcock and Brown pa-
tiently await a break in the
weather prior to the takeoff at Lester's field June 14.*
VICKERS LTD.

few bottles of beer were stowed aboard and the fliers squeezed into the cockpit, Brown on the left and Alcock on the right. Between them lay a big battery for heating their flying suits.

Wheel chocks and men leaning against the leading edge of the wings held the airplane in place as Alcock revved up the engines. A mechanic pulled the chocks, the men ducked under the wing, and the Vimy, moving slowly, began its uphill run. Some 1,200 feet ahead lay the flight's first obstacles—a stone wall and, just beyond, a low hill with pine woods. The Vimy gained speed and, with only 300 feet of field remaining, Alcock eased the heavy ship into the air. The wall and woods slipped by a scant few feet below. A side gust dropped the Vimy, but Alcock righted it in time.

On the ground, the onlookers thought the plane had crashed,

Just before takeoff, Alcock stows a thermos of hot chocolate aboard the Vimy.

VICKERS LTD.

for it vanished behind the hill. Soon, though, it came roaring back overhead, climbing steadily eastward over St. John's and out over the ocean. Now it was Alcock's and Brown's turn to match wits with the mighty Atlantic.

Even with the engines at half throttle for cruising, the men found conversation difficult in the noisy cockpit. There was little

Above: *With only 300 feet of field remaining, Alcock eases the fuel-heavy Vimy into the air. Ahead: 1,800 miles of open sea.*

Right: *Just after takeoff, the Vimy struggles for altitude as Alcock's skill averts a crash.*

time for talk, anyway. The unwieldy Vimy required Alcock's full attention. (His hands and feet never left the controls for an instant throughout the flight.) Brown kept busy reading engine dials and gauges (mounted on a strut behind him) and checking airspeed and altitude, in addition to his continual navigational duties. The latter caused pain in his lame leg, for he had to twist about and kneel on the seat to "shoot" the sun with his sextant, and bend far forward to sight the waves through a drift indicator under his feet. It soon became clear that the flight was a two-man task, and Alcock must have felt a sense of relief that he was not trying to do the whole job alone.

A brisk tailwind helped, but the clear skies gave way to dense fog after an hour or so—the first sign of how wrong the weather forecast had been. Flying blind, with even the wingtips obscured in the mist, Brown navigated by dead reckoning. He tapped his wireless key to send out a position report, but nothing happened. The transmitter was dead; a small propeller attached to a strut to drive a generator, had broken off, leaving no current for the transmitter. The world would receive no word from the Vimy for the rest of the flight.

By 6:00 P.M. (Greenwich Mean Time), Brown estimated they had flown about 200 miles. Alcock nosed the Vimy up, hoping to get above the clouds so that Brown could sight the sun and better estimate their position. Again they plunged into the mists as the Vimy climbed from a clear space below the clouds but above the fog.

Suddenly a noise like a machine gun burst from the port engine. The men watched in horror as an exhaust pipe split away, melted to white heat, and disappeared in the slipstream. Flames streamed aft from six exposed cylinders, but luckily stayed clear of struts and wing fabric. The noise, now deafening, made conversation almost impossible for the rest of the flight. To communicate, Brown scribbled notes and Alcock used hand signals.

Two hours out of St. John's, they ate some sandwiches. At

three hours and still in the mists they had reached 5,000 feet and Brown estimated they had covered 450 miles. Moisture was everywhere, adding to the discomfort of the open cockpit. An hour later, at 6,000 feet, they broke into the clear for a few minutes and Brown, looking aft, "shot" the sun, now low in the west. They were almost exactly on course.

At 9:30, darkness fell and the cold increased. Then the battery for their flying suits failed. Besides the cold, the night ahead promised other problems as the Vimy still cruised in the clouds, with Brown now hoping for a glimpse of the stars to help keep them on course.

Midnight (and June 15) found the Vimy eight hours out and climbing from one cloud layer to another, Alcock carefully running the engines at low throttle. They broke finally into a clear night sky, the moon and stars bright overhead. Brown took a reading and, his near-frozen fingers fumbling with flashlight and charts, calculated their position: slightly south of course, 977 miles covered at an average speed of 121 miles an hour. Halfway across and beyond the "point of no return," Alcock and Brown celebrated with sandwiches, chocolate, and coffee laced with whiskey.

The Vimy droned on, clouds towering high on both sides, and the cold increased—a minor annoyance compared to the near disasters that lay ahead. Shortly after 3:00 A.M., 11 hours out and with Ireland 600 miles ahead, the Vimy plunged into a black storm cloud. Rain, then hail, drove into the cockpit and lightning flashed around the plane, which was tossed about like a leaf in the turbulence. The instruments spun wildly and the Vimy, stalling at a height of 4,000 feet, fell into a steep spiral, plunging out of control toward the ocean invisible below.

The roaring engines told Alcock the ship was in a dive. He fought for control, throttling the racing engines, but the plunge continued. Under 1,000 feet and still with no sight of the sea, the fliers thought they were finished. Then, less than 100 feet above the water, they broke clear of the blackness. But the ocean was tilted vertically on one side, the sky on the other. The Vimy was tipped on its side, still headed for a crash. Alcock's piloting experience took over: instinctively he snapped the Vimy into level flight as the waves skimmed by a few feet below, the spray actually striking the lower wings. The compass showed them heading west, back toward Newfoundland. Alcock turned the ship around and climbed eastward, the storm now behind them. But they were not yet home free.

The Vimy hit another storm and found a new danger—snow, sleet, and ice. Alcock nosed the ship up, hoping for a glimpse of the rising sun, for it was now 5:00 A.M. At 9,000 feet the engines sputtered and lost power, starving for fuel as the air intakes became blocked with snow. Equally bad, the fuel intake gauges, which Brown had to read to regulate properly the flow of gasoline into the engines, became invisible under a coat of ice.

Now it was Brown's turn to save the flight. To avoid a complete power failure he climbed out of the cockpit onto the fuselage and then to the wing. Grasping a strut, he chipped at the ice with a jackknife, clearing the gauges despite the slipstream which threatened to hurl him into space at any moment. He turned to the air intakes on the port engine and cleared them, too, defying the whirling propeller and exhaust flames only inches away. The engine ran smoothly again. He did the same with the starboard engine, then dropped back into the cockpit, exhausted but successful. During the next hour, Brown had to return to the wings five more times to keep the Vimy airborne in the storm.

At 7:20 A.M., at an altitude of 11,000 feet, they broke out of the storm and saw the sun. Brown took a reading and estimated they were within an hour of sighting Ireland. The Vimy, aloft 15 hours, had covered over 1,800 miles of open sea. Only skill and courage had enabled Alcock and Brown to survive the two storms. Now, as they descended to warmer altitudes, their troubles were over—or so they thought.

The Vimy again became sheathed in ice. The controls were almost completely jammed and the starboard engine lost power, its radiator shutters locked solid in ice. The ship dropped into the clouds, as Alcock sought a warmer, clearer altitude near the sea. The engines heated up and Alcock reduced them to idling speed. The Vimy dropped through the clouds, almost silent except for the wind whistling through struts and wires. Below 5,000 feet the ice began to slide away and the controls became free. At 1,000 feet and still with no sign of the sea, Alcock and Brown, not fully trusting the altimeter, prepared to ditch. At 500 feet they dropped from the clouds, Alcock gunned the engines full throttle, and the Vimy levelled out at 200 feet.

Brown was fixing breakfast from the remaining food when Alcock, at 8:15 A.M., spotted two tiny islands and, farther ahead, mountains whose peaks were hidden in the clouds. A town came into view which Brown identified as Clifden in the county of Connemara. He saw the masts of a transatlantic Marconi wireless station which he knew was at Clifden. It was a drizzly Sunday morning as the Vimy crossed the coastline (at 8:25 A.M.) and swept low over the town, its noisy engines startling many townspeople and awaking others.

Having achieved their goal of a nonstop flight, Alcock and Brown decided to land rather than risk striking the cloud-covered mountains lying between them and England. Alcock chose a green stretch of land, dropped down, leveled out and too late realized they were over a swampy bog. The wheels hit, the mud sprayed over the ship, and the Vimy came to a stop, its nose deep in the mire and its tail pointing skyward. Alcock and Brown, smelling gasoline fumes and fearing fire, unhooked their seat belts and leaped unhurt from the cockpit. They turned to face the greetings of about a hundred townspeople who, cheering and shouting for autographs, half-carried the fliers to the wireless station.

Alcock's and Brown's historic flight covered 1,890 miles. Flying at an average speed of 118 miles an hour, they crossed the

VICKERS LTD.

A muddy Irish bog brought this end to the flight of Alcock and Brown.

Alcock and Brown had only a few feet to leap after the Vimy's nose buried itself deep in the mire near Clifden, Ireland.

VICKERS LTD.

VICKERS LTD.

Worldwide publicity and acclaim followed flight of Alcock and Brown.

At Holyhead, England, Alcock and Brown deliver the first mail to cross the Atlantic by plane.

Irish coastline 15 hours, 57 minutes after leaving the Newfoundland coast. Their total time from takeoff to landing was 16 hours, 12 minutes. The Vimy, badly damaged and stripped by souvenir hunters, never flew again.

Despite headlines, wild welcomes, official dinners, speeches, and a long list of honors, including knighthood, Alcock and Brown maintained a pleasant modesty. Their story ends sadly,

Winston Churchill, then Secretary of State for War, presents the $50,000 Daily Mail *prize to Alcock and Brown on June 20, 1919.*

Restored, the Vimy found its final home in the Science Museum, London, where it is a venerable and respected attraction.

though. Sir John Alcock was dead in six months. He crashed on a fogbound field in France while trying to fly a new Vickers Viking amphibian from London to Paris. Sir Arthur Whitten Brown, crushed by the death of his friend, quit aviation and devoted his time to engineering. He died in 1948, heartbroken over the loss of his only son in the World War II Battle of Arnhem.

Only the Vimy remains. Retrieved from the bog and rebuilt, it may still be seen in the Science Museum in London, mute testimony to one of the most significant and dramatic flights in aviation history, an achievement which took place only sixteen years after the Wright brothers' first flight!

3 THE R-34

One Airship, Four Firsts _____

HEAVIER-THAN-AIR machines—airplanes and, to a far lesser degree, helicopters—dominate aviation today. Lighter-than-air vehicles (airships), which once held great promise, have all but vanished from the skies. Dirigibles (airships with rigid structures) have been gone for more than four decades, while blimps (nonrigid airships) survive chiefly for sight-seeing and as advertising aids. Balloons, going only where the wind goes, remain as the occasionally spectacular hobby of sportsmen, but with zero value for reliable transportation.

Thus, it may surprise some in this age of the jet to learn that it was an airship which made the first east-to-west air crossing of the Atlantic, as well as the first round-trip ocean flight. In 1919

The German dirigible, Graf Zeppelin, *made 144 trips across the Atlantic between 1928 and 1937.*

the British dirigible, R-34, flew to New York and back, each of the nonstop flights having covered well over 3,500 miles. Aboard was the ship's 30-man crew plus (on the east-west hop) a stowaway. The flights were, of course, the first transatlantic crossings by dirigible, with the outbound flight being the first nonstop crossing from east to west—in all a total of four firsts for the R-34.

The R-34 and such later giants as the *Hindenburg* and the *Graf Zeppelin* and the U.S. Navy's *Akron* and *Macon* were among the last of their line. Their ancestors of the distant past were the hydrogen and hot air balloons of the late 1700s and 1800s, followed by the remarkable airships of the Brazilian, Alberto Santos-Dumont, who made many historic flights in France in the late 1800s and early 1900s.

Their immediate ancestors were the graceful airships of Count Ferdinand von Zeppelin, the German inventor (in 1900) of the first successful rigid airship, whose "zeppelins" ruled the lighter-than-air scene for over a quarter century. During World War I the Zeppelin company built almost 100 rigid airships. Flying by night, the huge craft bombed British cities and industries from altitudes up to 20,000 feet. Many were lost as their hydrogen flamed instantly when hit by bullets from British fighters or by small bombs dropped from planes flying just above them. Slow speed, vulnerability to wind and weather, and a series of accidents, climaxed by the explosion of the *Hindenburg* on May 6, 1937, combined to end the saga of the dirigible.

The R-34, a close copy of the German L-3 "super zeppelins" of World War I, was 643 feet long with a maximum diameter of 79 feet and an overall height of 92 feet. Five Sunbeam Maori engines of 250 horsepower each (and of uniform unreliability) were suspended in gondolas beneath the giant hull, driving the R-34 along at a cruise speed of 45 miles an hour.

The hull, a framework of Duralumin girders and bracing wires, held 19 huge hydrogen-filled gasbags. Linen fabric, doped to give a smooth, airtight surface, covered the framework. Control surfaces—vertical fins and rudders and horizontal stabilizers and elevators—also of Duralumin and linen, were mounted at the extreme aft end of the airship.

The forward gondola, suspended like the others on struts beneath the hull, housed a large control cabin and one engine. Two more engines were slung amidships in parallel gondolas. Farther aft, the final gondola housed emergency controls and two engines geared to drive a single large propeller. Ranged along a keel and catwalk within the hull were the crew's quarters where hammocks, shelves, plate racks, and collapsible furniture vied for space with fuel tanks, water ballast bags, and parachutes. Ladders, exposed to the slipstream, led to the gondolas below.

The R-34 was one of the several aircraft competing in 1919 for the $50,000 *Daily Mail* prize, and might well have won it except for a freak accident during its first flight, March 24. Over the Irish Sea, the control wires to the tail somehow became displaced, the ship tilted sharply, nose up, and two fuel tanks tore loose, ripping through the linen fabric and plunging into the sea. Lightened, the ship soared to 8,000 feet, nose pointed skyward, and only skilled airmanship brought the craft under control and back to her base. Unluckily, however, the water ballast, frozen at the high altitude, could not be jettisoned before landing. The result was a hard landing which pushed the rear gondola through the fabric and up into the hull.

The R-34 did not fly again until late May and it was not until the morning of July 2, following several test flights, that she took off for New York from her base at East Fortune, in Scotland. Both the NC-4 and the Vimy, as we have seen, had already made their historic flights. But the difficult east-west crossing against the westerly headwinds remained as a challenge for the R-34. With very little available in the way of communications and weather equipment, and with low-powered and generally unreliable engines, the venture, in the words of the R-34's engineer officer, "offered little more than an even chance for survival."

Major George Herbert Scott, an airship veteran of five years experience, was in command as the R-34 lifted heavily into a misty sky at 1:42 A.M. and quickly disappeared into the low-hanging clouds. The liftoff and early hours of the flight were critical because the airship, carrying her maximum payload of fuel (4,900 gallons), men, and equipment, was overloaded by about a ton, despite hydrogen bags filled to their limit. Barely able to lift from the ground, the ship needed the added thrust of her five engines to drive her up into the clouds. Ahead, invisible to the crew, lay the Scottish hills.

Airships must constantly fight a delicate battle to maintain their best altitude. If forced to fly high to avoid hills or rough air, the decreased air pressure causes the precious hydrogen to

The R-34 dirigible in flight at the Beardmore factory at Inchinnon, England, in 1919.

escape through automatic valves. In sunlight, the hydrogen, heated, expands and also escapes. In rain and mist, the gas contracts and this, along with moisture collecting on the huge fabric envelope, causes loss of lift. To correct the latter condition a dirigible, especially an overloaded craft such as the R-34, must tilt its nose sharply up to remain airborne. But the increased flight angle means slower speeds and higher fuel con-

Major Scott in the R-34's control cabin prior to the flight.

sumption, a situation which added to the anxiety of Scott and his crew.

Other problems also plagued the R-34. The engines, already giving trouble, had to be rested and worked on periodically. Fortunately, a tailwind boosted the ship along at ground speeds up to 65 miles an hour during the first few hundred miles. As a result, it was possible to shut down three engines and use only the pair amidships for a while, thus saving fuel. But over the Atlantic with 2,000 miles of open ocean ahead, headwinds showed up as expected, reducing the ship's ground speed substantially. (The R-34's average air speed of 42 miles an hour became a ground speed of only 33 miles an hour for the east-to-west flight.)

The 30-man crew, mostly Royal Air Force although the R-34 was a Naval airship, was divided into two watches. Included under Major Scott were a second and third officer, an engineering officer, navigator, weather officer, and an assortment of coxwains, riggers, telegraphers, and engine technicians. Also included, for "special duties," were Brigadier General E. M. Maitland, Britain's senior airship officer, and Major J.E.M.

Crew of the R-34, showing 28 of the 31 persons aboard for the transatlantic flight. Seated, center, is Major George Herbert Scott, airship commander.

Pritchard, technical observer and photographer. Aboard as representative of the U.S. Navy was Lieutenant Commander Zachary Landsdowne. Often as many as ten or twelve of these men were crowded into the forward control car, nerve center of the ship, where a large altimeter—a dirigible's most important instrument—hung in full view of all.

By 9:00 A.M. the R-34 was flying between cloud layers. Later the sun broke through and Scott, fearing overheating of the hydrogen and wishing to conserve all possible lift for the long flight ahead, brought the ship down into the cool mist below. The navigator, unable to see the ocean horizon, climbed a long ladder up through the ship's girders to the top of the hull. There, he took a reading on the distant cloud horizon, his head and shoulders riding just out of the mist, although the ship itself was covered.

The riggers went topside, too, inspecting and repairing the gasbags, the outer envelope, and the gas valves. At times they had to walk nearly 200 yards along the top of the hull, exposed to the air blast and with only a hand rope to keep them from being swept overboard.

The men ate their meals in two sittings. However, fifteen together in the forward dining quarters caused the ship to nose down, so some had to carry their food far aft and eat on the narrow walkway above the keel.

The stowaway was found on the first afternoon: William Ballantyne, a technician, dropped from the crew list at the last moment to make room for one of the VIPs, had hidden high in the girders between two gasbags. But sickened by the escaping gas, he descended to hide in the keel where he was soon spotted. With the ship now over the ocean, General Maitland could not send Ballantyne over the side by parachute; the stowaway worked his passage as a cook and by pumping fuel to the engines. A second "stowaway" was found later in the keel, a tiger cat named Wopsie, smuggled aboard as the ship's mascot.

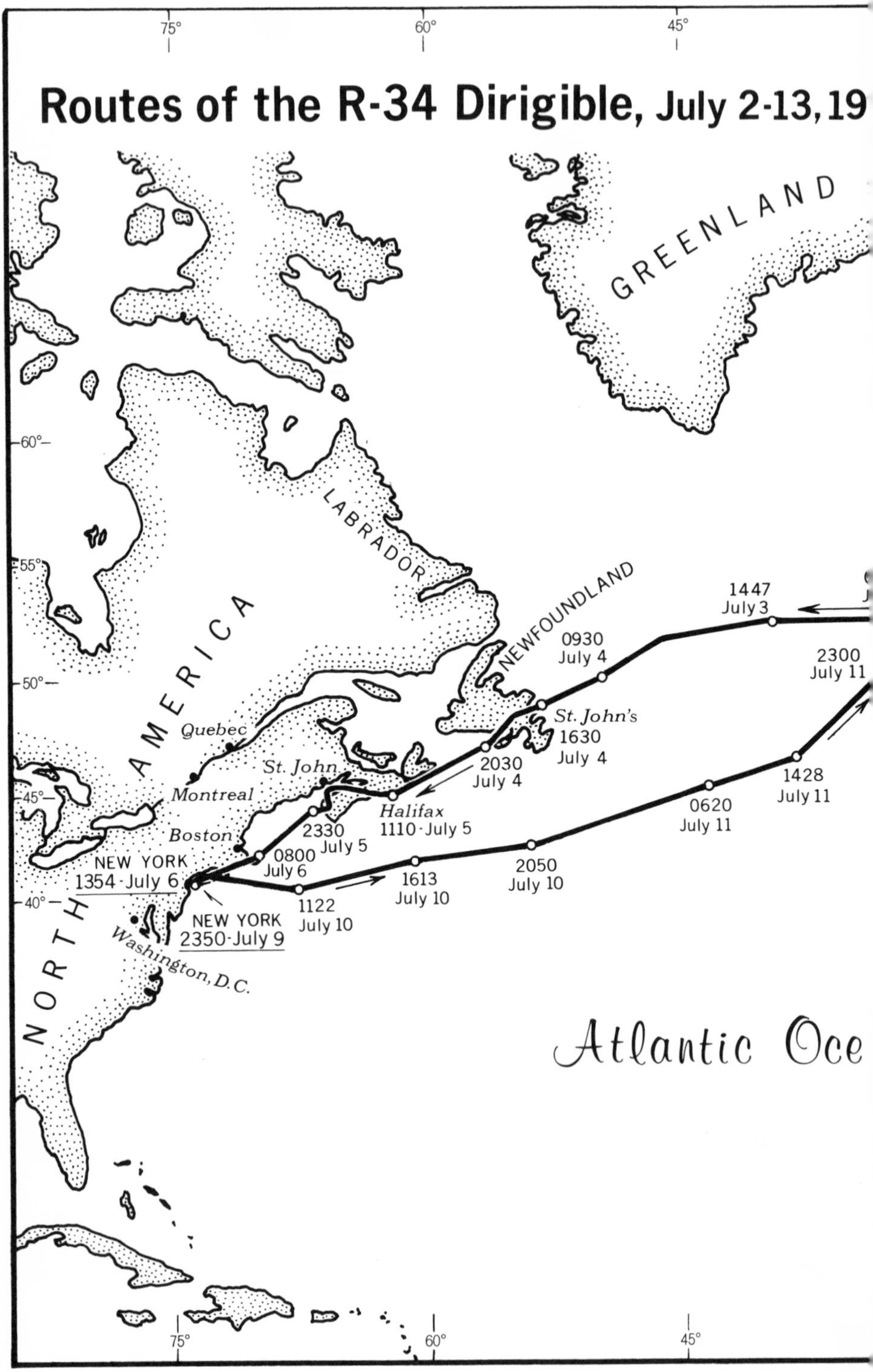
Routes of the R-34 Dirigible, July 2-13,19
75°
60°
45°
GREENLAND
LABRADOR
NEWFOUNDLAND
NORTH AMERICA
60°
55°
50°
45°
40°
1447
July 3
0930
July 4
2300
July 11
St. John's
1630
July 4
2030
July 4
1428
July 11
Quebec
St. John
Montreal
Halifax
1110-July 5
0620
July 11
Boston
2330
July 5
0800
July 6
NEW YORK
1354-July 6
2050
July 10
1613
July 10
1122
July 10
NEW YORK
2350-July 9
Washington, D.C.
Atlantic Oce

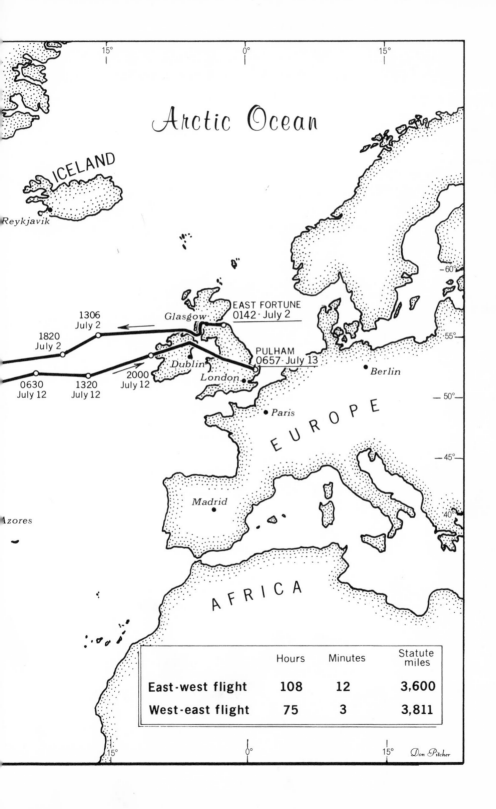

Arctic Ocean

ICELAND

Reykjavik

EAST FORTUNE
0142 · July 2

1306
July 2

Glasgow

1820
July 2

PULHAM
0657 · July 13

Dublin

2000
July 12

London

0630
July 12

1320
July 12

Berlin

Paris

EUROPE

Madrid

Azores

AFRICA

	Hours	Minutes	Statute miles
East-west flight	**108**	**12**	**3,600**
West-east flight	**75**	**3**	**3,811**

Don Pitcher

Throughout the day the R-34 cruised above a solid cloud layer, the sea visible only occasionally for a minute at a time. Scott reduced the engines to half speed, just to keep them running. Riding at 3,000 feet, the ship plunged in and out of the clouds. Cold air at that height brought a loss of lift and all five engines had to be run at near full power with the dirigible's nose sharply up to maintain altitude. But speed dropped and fuel consumption increased, so Scott ordered the ship down to a lower, warmer altitude where the flight continued through the night.

The next morning (July 3), found the R-34 almost halfway across the ocean and about 24 hours from Newfoundland. Even the fuel problem looked better. Then the headwinds increased and, later in the day, a storm began to carry the airship north of her course. Fifty-mile-an-hour winds forced the craft to fly almost sideways to stay near the course and a cold rain seeped into the control car, soaking the charts. More serious, the rain added weight to the already moist fabric of the hull. Thanks to the lessening load of fuel, however, the ship was able to nose up and climb above the storm. She rode smoothly all night at a height of about 3,400 feet.

The skies had cleared by the following morning (July 4) and the men saw their first icebergs. Soon the sea was dotted with the towering bergs and broken pack ice. Scott now cruised the R-34 at a height of 4,000 feet, finding that to be the best altitude, with the ship's changing conditions of lift and fuel, to maintain level flight. At 12:50 P.M. local time they sighted land—small islands off the north coast of Newfoundland—and 40 minutes later, 60 hours after leaving the Irish coast, they were over Trinity Bay, Newfoundland. The R-34 had reached the North American continent.

This good news was tempered by bad: fuel consumption had increased and the possibility of reaching New York nonstop was becoming less and less certain, for strong headwinds were expected along the American east coast.

The R-34 droned on all day, crossing the bleak Newfoundland wilderness, the Gulf of St. Lawrence, and, on July 5, Nova Scotia. The hazards increased: buffeting gales forced the ship dangerously low over Nova Scotia. Later, with the fuel load lessening rapidly, the ship had too much lift and had to be taken to a higher altitude to valve off hydrogen. The skilled handling of hydrogen, gasoline, and water ballast would be more vital than ever for the remainder of the flight.

A thunderstorm overtook the ship over the Bay of Fundy. In a terrifying few minutes the dirigible plunged hundreds of feet in one drop, pitched and tossed. Loose objects went clattering about the ship. The skies cleared but that evening came the worst turbulence of the whole flight. Again the ship was tossed about, nose up, then nose down, the huge craft twisting under the onslaught until it seemed her frame would break apart. For the crew, the experience was as surprising as frightening, for the sky was clear and the sea calm.

The fuel problem remained and Scott reluctantly radioed authorities in New York that he would have to land the R-34 at Montauk on the eastern end of Long Island to refuel. But tail-winds appeared during the night and sped the ship along off the Massachusetts coast and on Sunday morning (July 6, the fifth day aloft) the Long Island shore loomed ahead.

The crew rechecked the fuel supply, collecting the last drops from the ship's 81 tanks. Passing Montauk, Scott decided to try for Hazelhurst Field, Mineola, the original goal, without stopping. He won his gamble, but only barely: when the R-34 touched down at Mineola at 9:54 A.M., all drinking water and most of the food were gone, the gasbags hung slack, and only 140 gallons of gasoline remained—enough for a mere two more hours of flight.

Two minor "firsts" had been recorded: as the R-34 hovered before landing, Major Pritchard parachuted from the ship to direct an inexperienced ground crew, thus becoming the first air arrival from overseas to set foot in the United States and the

The R-34 landing at Mineola, New York, July 5, 1919.

U.S. Army personnel gather around the forward gondola after the R-34's landing on July 5, 1919.

An inexperienced American ground crew hauled the R-34 to earth at Mineola, New York.

The history-making British dirigible drew crowds during its stay at Hazelhurst Field, Mineola, Long Island, New York.

only foreigner to arrive in the U.S. by parachute.

The R-34's journey had taken 108 hours, 12 minutes, a world aircraft endurance record. Scott and his men received a thunderous welcome from the thousands gathered at Mineola and were wined and dined as heroes for four days in New York City. Just before midnight, July 9, the R-34 took off for home. To repay New York's hospitality, the ship was flown over Manhattan Island, her silver bulk caught in the beams of searchlights from the metropolis. Floating at 2,000 feet, she stayed safely clear of the tallest skyscraper, the 790-foot Woolworth Building.

Turning east, the R-34 moved at a surface speed of 80 miles an hour, carried along by the westerly trade winds. By morning, the ship was 400 miles at sea and rushing eastward at 90 miles an hour, even with one engine shut down.

Aboard to help with the balky engines were two additional engineers. Left behind were a wireless operator and the stowaway, Ballantyne, who went home by sea with the ground crew. Lieutenant Colonel W. N. Hensley, representing the U.S. Army, replaced Lieutenant Commander Landsdowne.

Clear weather and favorable winds continued all day, and the second night was like the first—uneventful and smooth. So well was the flight progressing that Scott and Maitland changed the

Crowds gather at Mineola, New York, to view the R-34 after the west-to-east flight July 2–6, 1919.

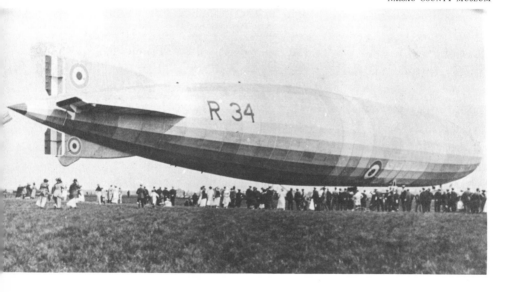

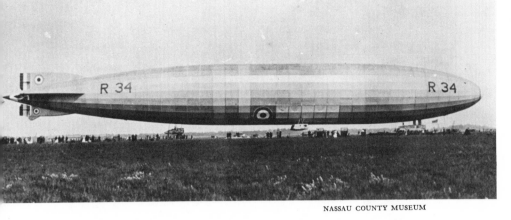

The R-34's 643-foot length is seen in this view of the dirigible at Mineola. Picture was taken July 9, 1919, the day the R-34 took off for its return trip to England.

R-34 being prepared for the return crossing. Foreground, hydrogen gas containers used to refill the 19 huge gasbag

flight plan to include a circle over London before flying to the base at East Fortune. This change was abandoned on Friday morning when one of the two engines in the aft car failed, with damage too bad for repairs in flight.

Clouds rolled in to cover the sea from horizon to horizon. At one point Scott dropped the ship through five separate cloud layers, seeking a view of the ocean in order to fix the ship's position. At 900 feet and with still no view of the water, he took the ship up again above the cloud layers.

Nearing home, the R-34 began receiving messages from a wireless station on the Irish coast. One message, relayed from the Navy, ordered Scott to land at Pulham, in England, rather than at the ship's East Fortune base in Scotland. This would add four hours flight time to an airship already handicapped by low power. (Later, some people believed that the change was ordered by officials who favored heavier-than-air craft over the costly dirigibles and who wished to sidetrack the ceremonies and publicity which awaited the R-34's arrival at East Fortune.)

Only two of her five engines were in running condition when the R-34 reached Pulham, England, at the end of the round-trip crossing.

VICKERS LTD.

The R-34 lands at Pulham, England, to complete its round-trip crossing of the Atlantic July 13, 1919.

The R-34 reached the Irish coast near the two small islands which Alcock and Brown had seen when they dropped from the fog two months before. The mountains and flatland of northern Ireland, then Belfast and the Irish Sea slipped by beneath and the airship crossed the English coast near Liverpool during the night. She continued across England, coming to earth at Pulham at 6:57 A.M., July 13. At touchdown, only two engines were in running condition, the engine trouble continuing to the end.

The return trip, covering 3,811 miles (over 200 miles longer than the east-west crossing) was much faster, being completed in 75 hours, 3 minutes, or exactly 3 days, 3 hours, and 3 minutes. The R-34's surface speed on the homeward flight averaged just over 50 miles an hour, compared to 33 miles an hour for the outward voyage.

Six months later, during a stormy winter night, the R-34, through a series of communications and navigational errors, struck a hill while on a training flight. Damaged, she bounced back into the air and many hours later struggled back to her base on two engines. In the early hours of the next morning, however, while moored at the base and awaiting transfer into her hangar, she was destroyed by gale winds. The gallant airship's sad end seems symbolic of the ultimate disappearance of dirigibles from the aviation scene.

4 THE DOUGLAS WORLD

First East-to

CRUISERS
-West Crossing by Airplane ————————

THE TWO U.S. ARMY biplanes groped through the fog at 90 miles an hour only 50 feet or less above the icy waters of the North Atlantic, heading west somewhere between Iceland and Greenland.

Four helmeted fliers peered anxiously through their goggles from the open cockpits of the low-flying seaplanes. They were Lieutenants Lowell H. Smith and Leslie P. Arnold in the *Chicago* and Lieutenants Erik H. Nelson and John Harding, Jr., in the *New Orleans*. They were four of the Army's very best pilots. Yet they knew it would take all their skills and courage to stay alive in the longest and most dangerous flight they'd ever attempted—835 miles across an ocean beset with icebergs and headwinds in addition to the blinding fog.

The Douglas World Cruiser, Boston, *is hoisted ashore at Dutch Harbor, Alaska, for an engine change, nine days after start of world flight.*

Now, 75 miles from Greenland, they found themselves among a seemingly endless expanse of huge icebergs. Their terror increased by the minute. Forced to fly as low as 30 feet to keep on course in the fog, they barely had time to see the giant bergs and decide which way to turn to avoid crashing into them. Three times they came upon the icy monsters so suddenly that they had time only to pull back on the control wheel and zoom up into the even denser fog above. Then, flying blind, they groped their way back down to the sea, praying that the surface would be clear enough to give them a few seconds to look around before resuming their deadly game of tag and leapfrog with the towers of ice.

The date was August 21, 1924, and the *Chicago* and the *New Orleans* were two of four World Cruisers specially built for the Army Air Service to attempt the first round-the-world flight. Designed by a young engineer, Donald Douglas, the planes were built in the Douglas factory at Santa Monica, California. Each was 38 feet long with a wingspan of 50 feet and each was powered with a 400-horsepower, 12-cylinder Liberty engine. The pilot sat in the front cockpit between the wings. The copilot-mechanic occupied a rear cockpit and behind him was a large baggage and tool compartment. For overland flights the Cruisers were fitted with wheels and tail skids. For over-water legs the wheels were replaced by twin pontoons.

The Cruisers had begun their world flight April 6 at Seattle, Washington. On April 30, on the flight's fourth leg, the flagship *Seattle* became lost in fog and crashed on a mountainside in the Aleutians. On August 2, the *Boston* was forced down in the Atlantic between Scotland and Iceland and sank during a salvage attempt. (The crews of both lost planes escaped unhurt and eventually were rescued.)

Only the *Chicago* and the *New Orleans* had survived, and now they too were in serious trouble. The historic journey, which already had covered almost 20,000 miles by way of Alaska, the Aleutians, Japan, the Asian continent, and Europe—

Equipped with wheels for overland flight, the three World Cruisers are warmed up prior to a takeoff. As seaplanes, the New Orleans *and* Chicago *made the first air crossing of the Atlantic east to west.*

spanning seas, mountains, jungles, deserts, farms, and cities—
seemed about to end as a failure in the foggy North Atlantic.
The fliers knew that the Atlantic would be their toughest obstacle, and it was proving to be just that.

The *Boston, Chicago*, and *New Orleans* had flown from England to the Orkney Islands north of Scotland on July 30. That
put them on the edge of the Atlantic, ready for the first hazardous leap westward, a 550-mile flight to the village of Hornafjord on the southeast coast of Iceland. Navy vessels stationed
along the route reported bad weather, so it was not until
August 2 that the three Cruisers took off from the Orkneys.
Within minutes they ran into thick fog, a rain squall, and more
fog. After that, each experienced its own separate adventure.

As the three planes climbed up through the fog to get on top
of the weather, the *New Orleans* became caught in the propeller
wash of one of the other planes and fell into a spin. As if by a
miracle, Nelson managed to halt the spin just above the water
with only seconds to spare. As it leveled out, the *New Orleans*
flew into a clear spot. Nelson and Harding were then lucky
enough to fly under the fog until they were completely out of it.
They circled about, looking for the *Chicago* and *Boston*. Seeing
neither plane, they resumed their flight, flew for hours over a fog
bank, and eventually landed in the bay off Hornafjord. Ashore,
they joined some Navy men who had rigged up a temporary
radio station. Then they waited for the *Chicago* and *Boston* to
join them.

Meanwhile, Smith and Arnold in the *Chicago* and Lieutenants
Leigh Wade and Henry H. Ogden in the *Boston* had climbed to
2,500 feet and gotten above the fog and rain. They circled for 20
minutes, wondering if Nelson and Harding had crashed into the
sea or had flown on. They then returned to their base at Kirk-
wall in the Orkneys, thinking it better to report the *New Orleans'* disappearance immediately rather than waiting the six to
eight hours it would take to reach Iceland. A few hours later

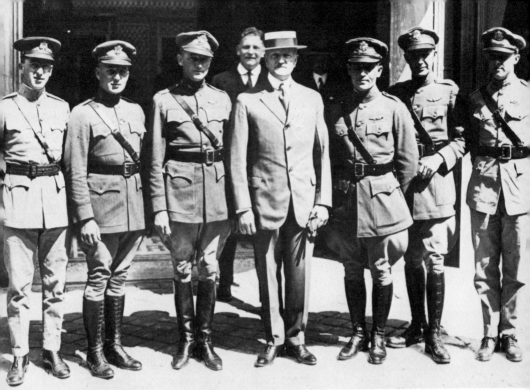

Prior to the transatlantic flight, crew members of the Chicago, Boston, *and* New Orleans *pose with General Pershing in Paris, July 15, 1924. Left to right: Lieutenants Ogden, Arnold, Smith; General Pershing; Lieutenants Wade, Nelson, and Harding.*

they received the good news in a wireless report from Nelson that the *New Orleans* had just missed disaster, but had reached Iceland safely.

The next morning, the *Chicago* and *Boston* took off again for Iceland. The weather was clear, but trouble struck an hour and a half later: the *Boston*, suddenly powerless, turned into the wind and glided to a landing in the ocean, Wade setting the seaplane down safely despite high waves and a heavy swell. The *Chicago* circled low over the downed plane, but Wade signaled Smith and Arnold not to land but to continue their flight, realizing that if the *Chicago* landed it would be unable to take off in the heavy seas.

Smith and Arnold headed the *Chicago* for the Faroe Islands
100 miles away where they dropped a message to the destroyer
Billingsby, giving the *Boston*'s position, time of landing, and the
wind and sea conditions. The destroyer radioed the cruiser
Richmond and both headed for the *Boston* at full speed. The *Chicago* continued on to Iceland, flying the final 300 miles through
fog and drizzle at a height of 50 feet, and moored alongside the
New Orleans in the harbor at Hornafjord.

Bobbing about in the rough seas, Wade and Ogden in the
Boston settled down to await rescue. A drop in engine oil pressure from normal to zero in a few seconds, apparently from
failure of the oil pump, had forced them down. They guessed
they were midway between the Orkneys and the Faroes. As the
hours passed they worried about the plane's seaworthiness, for a
pontoon and struts had been damaged in the landing. A sea gull
arrived and floated close to the plane, seemingly as lonesome as
the two aviators.

A wisp of smoke appeared on the horizon. A boat! Maybe
rescue was at hand. Ogden fired flares from the top wing, but
the boat vanished below the horizon without seeing them. They
realized then what a speck they were in the ocean. Rain and fog
closed in, the wind increased, and the gull departed.

More hours passed and finally another wisp of smoke was seen
on the horizon. With a flag improvised from the *Boston*'s wood
and fabric fuselage, the fliers wigwagged frantically from the
plane's top wing. They fired more flares. This time they were
seen and a fishing trawler soon pulled alongside and took the
plane in tow. But, pitching about in the wind and waves, the
seaplane was too much of a burden for the little trawler. Making
no headway, they decided to drift and await one of the Naval
vessels.

It was late in the afternoon when both the *Billingsby* and the
Richmond arrived. Wade and Ogden boarded the *Richmond*
and watched as an attempt was made to hoist the *Boston*

The Boston *being hoisted aboard the U.S.S.* Richmond. *The boom broke, breaking the propeller and putting a hole in a pontoon, which later caused the plane to sink.*

aboard. But a block and tackle slipped and the plane dropped into the water, badly damaging its pontoons. Sailors from the cruiser worked all night to keep the *Boston* afloat, slowly towing it toward the Faroes. But at 5:00 A.M., only a mile from shore, the battered seaplane capsized and sank.

On August 5, the *Chicago* and *New Orleans* continued westward from Hornafjord to Reykjavik, the capital of Iceland, a 290-mile hop. They followed the coastline against headwinds so strong that at times they crept along at only a few miles an hour. Rough seas prevented a landing in the clear outer harbor, but skilled piloting enabled the fliers to set their planes down in a small area back of a breakwater, despite the presence of hundreds of boats which had sought shelter there. Reykjavik's popu-

The New Orleans *on the beach to dry at Reykjavik, Iceland.*

lation of about 25,000 lined the breakwater to welcome the world fliers.

At Reykjavik the crews prepared for the hazardous flight ahead. They made sure their planes were in the best possible condition and reduced weight by off-loading many tools and all extra clothing. They abandoned their original plan to fly to Angmassalik on Greenland's east coast, 500 miles away, when reports showed that ice along that coast would make landing impossible. Instead, they planned a far longer flight, 835 miles, around the southern tip of Greenland to Fredricksdal on the west coast, facing Labrador across Davis Strait. Besides the hazards of ice, fog, and gales, the course was entirely off the steamship lanes, which added to the risks of a forced landing.

Earthbound for over two weeks by bad weather reports, the *Chicago* and *New Orleans* took off for Greenland just before seven o'clock on the morning of August 21. (Accompanying them was a Dornier-Wal flying boat, a twin-engined, all-metal monoplane of the Italian Air Service, which also was attempting the first east-west crossing. The speedier monoplane pulled away from the two biplanes and soon disappeared over the horizon. However, it turned out to be a "hare and tortoise" race: the Italian pilot, Lieutenant Antonio Locatelli, fearing the fog and icebergs, later landed in the sea to await clearer weather. The plane was badly damaged in the landing. On August 24, Locatelli and his three-man crew were picked up by the American cruiser, *Richmond*.)

The Americans, as we saw earlier, chose to risk the near-blind flight among the icebergs. Approaching Greenland, the two planes finally became separated when the *Chicago* banked steeply to the right to avoid a mountainous iceberg ahead, while the *New Orleans* swung left. Smith and Arnold in the *Chicago* headed toward shore, while Nelson and Harding turned out to sea, each crew thinking the other had probably crashed into the berg.

After an hour of flying through the fog, dodging towers of ice on one side and rocky cliffs on the other, Smith and Arnold were forced to climb to 1,500 feet to clear a solid wall of fog ahead.

The three World Cruisers arrive over New York. They later completed their world flight at Seattle, Washington, September 28, 1924.

U.S. AIR FORCE

The New Orleans, *after refurbishing, stands ready for enshrinement in the Air Force Museum at Wright-Patterson AFB, Dayton, Ohio.*

Opposite: *The* New Orleans *on permanent display at the Air Force Museum in Dayton, Ohio, with sculptures of the six round-the-world fliers.*

The Chicago *on display at the Air and Space Museum, Smithsonian Institution, Washington, D.C.*

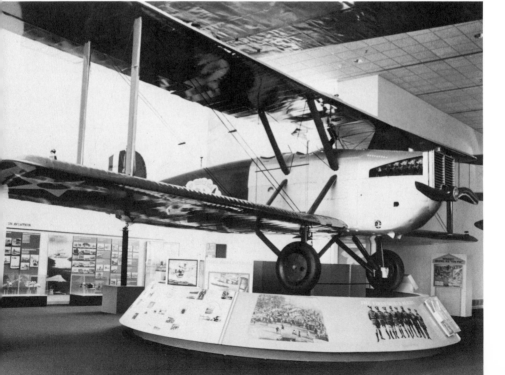

By sheer luck they finally found a hole in the clouds and spiraled down to a landing at Fredricksdal alongside a Danish Coast Guard cutter. Forty minutes later the *New Orleans* spotted the same opening and landed nearby. A pontoon slightly damaged by a big wave as the *New Orleans* touched down seemed of no consequence at all compared with the terrible 11-hour flight that the two seaplanes had survived.

On August 31, the two World Cruisers covered the 560 miles from Greenland to Labrador in mostly clear weather. They'd finally reached the North American continent. The Atlantic had been crossed for the first time by an airplane flying east to west.

The *Chicago* and *New Orleans* reached Seattle on September 28, 1924, the fliers receiving heroes' welcomes all the way across the United States. With them, and equally acclaimed, flew the new *Boston II*, which the Air Service had sent to Nova Scotia so that Wade and Ogden could complete the journey that had been interrupted through no fault of their own.

Thus ended the first round-the-world flight, a trip covering 26,345 miles in a total elapsed time of 176 days—only six days short of six months.

5 LINDBERGH

The Lone Eagle's Solo Classic ____

JOHN ALCOCK AND Arthur Whitten Brown, June 14–15, 1919. Charles A. Lindbergh, May 20–21, 1927. The achievements of these aviators, occurring less than eight years apart, stirred mankind's imagination more than any flight before or since. As a result, these twin ventures, especially Lindbergh's, loom above all others in moving aviation from infancy to maturity.

The flights were alike in several ways. Both were nonstop. In both, the fliers were competing for cash prizes as "dark horses," starting almost hopelessly late behind other competitors. Both defied the disappearances of earlier planes attempting the Atlantic crossing. Lindbergh, like Alcock and Brown, won honors and fame beyond his wildest dreams. And in both cases the heroes later found their fame tarnished by tragedy and sadness.

The dissimilarities were equally striking. The Britishers flew as a team which, as we have seen, saved the flight from disaster. The American relied on himself alone. The Vimy, a biplane and large for its time, had two water-cooled engines. Lindbergh's monoplane, a relatively small craft, used a single air-cooled engine. Alcock and Brown flew 1,890 miles, Lindbergh nearly twice as far—3,610 miles. The Britishers crash-landed in an Irish bog in daylight, content to have been the first to fly the ocean nonstop. The American made a night landing, setting his plane down at his precise destination, Le Bourget Field, Paris, intact and ready to fly again.

A $25,000 prize offered by Raymond Orteig, a wealthy New York hotel owner, had been in effect since 1919. The money was to go "to the first aviator who shall cross the Atlantic in a land or water aircraft (heavier-than-air) from Paris or the shores of France to New York or from New York to Paris or the shores of France, without a stop." This award and the glory of being first attracted several leading fliers and aircraft builders of the 1920s.

The first attempt for the prize ended in tragedy. On September 21, 1926, a three-engined Sikorsky S-35 sesquiplane, overloaded and also burdened with an untested auxiliary landing gear (to have been dropped once the plane became airborne), crashed and burned on takeoff at Roosevelt Field, New York. The pilot, French war ace René Fonck, and his copilot, U.S. Navy Lieutenant Lawrence Curtin, escaped unhurt, but the radio operator, Charles Clavier, and a Sikorsky mechanic, Jacob Islamoff, died in the flames.

Fall and winter weather prevented further attempts that year, but by early 1927 several competitors were well along in their preparations. An early favorite was a big Keystone biplane named the *American Legion*. This three-engined plane, a converted Army bomber, was built at Bristol, Pennsylvania, by the Huff-Daland Company. It was to be flown by Navy Lieutenant

The Columbia *flies over Long Island, New York, while setting a new world endurance record of 51 hours, 11 minutes. With Clarence Chamberlin and Bert Acosta at the controls, it was preparation for a transatlantic attempt.*

Commander Noel Davis who had been thinking of a transatlantic flight for almost two years. In mid-1926 Davis selected a Navy friend, Lieutenant Stanton H. (Bob) Wooster, as his co-pilot. By April, 1927, the *American Legion* was undergoing very encouraging test flights.

Another favorite was Commander Richard E. Byrd, already famous for the first flight over the North Pole, a claim which some critics now believe was a fraud in view of the limited speed and range of Byrd's plane, an early-model Fokker trimotor. By April, Byrd was testing a new Fokker trimotor, the *America*, for a New York-Paris flight with a crew of three.

The strongest entry, the Bellanca monoplane *Columbia*, suffered from human problems. Its owner, Charles E. Levine, a millionaire dealer in war surplus ammunition, who was neither a pilot nor a navigator, argued almost constantly with his pilots and others preparing for the flight. They seemed unable to agree on anything—the best route to fly, whether to carry the added weight of a radio, or whether the pilots should be covered by

life insurance. Levine refused to say which two of his three
pilots—Clarence Chamberlin, Bert Acosta, and Lloyd Bertaud
—would make the flight.

These and other problems, including legal action by Bertaud
against Levine, delayed the *Columbia*'s takeoff for Paris. From
an aviation viewpoint this was unfortunate because the *Columbia*, thanks to Bellanca's use of wing-shaped struts and fuselage,
was the most efficient plane in the race. In early April, with
pilots Chamberlin and Acosta, the *Columbia* set a new world
endurance record of 51 hours, 11 minutes (covering over 5,000
miles), far more than enough for a New York-Paris flight.

In France two war aces, Charles Nungesser and François Coli,
were completing preparations for a Paris-New York flight. Their
plane, a Levasseur biplane, finished in gleaming white paint and
named *L'Oiseau Blanc* (the *White Bird*), had a single 450-horse-
power engine and one open cockpit for the pilot (Nungesser)
and the navigator (Coli). The landing gear could be dropped
after takeoff to give higher speeds, while the lower fuselage sec-

*In the hectic days prior to his transatlantic flight with Charles A.
Levine, Clarence Chamberlin poses in the cockpit of the* Columbia.

The Levasseur biplane, L'Oiseau Blanc (*the* White Bird), *in which the French fliers, Nungesser and Coli, were lost in May, 1927.*

tion was shaped like a seaplane hull. The plan was to land the plane in New York Harbor upon completion of the flight. The *White Bird*'s maximum range of 4,000 miles did not allow much margin for fighting the headwinds of the east-west crossing, nor for errors in navigation in the 3,600-mile flight.

Onto this scene stepped a young airmail pilot and ex-barnstormer, twenty-five-year-old Charles Augustus Lindbergh. For several months, the lanky Lindbergh, then an Army Reserve captain, had been trying without success to obtain a plane for a New York-Paris flight. Among the companies turning him down was the Wright Corporation, Paterson, New Jersey, chiefly an engine manufacturer, but also builder of the Wright-Bellanca monoplane obtained later by Levine.

Desperate and with time running out, Lindbergh and a group of St. Louis, Missouri, businessmen began negotiating with Ryan, a small airplane company in San Diego, California. Ryan, they found, could build a plane for $6,000 (plus $4,000 for an engine) with delivery within four months. This looked good until Levine, who had founded the Columbia Aircraft Corporation by buying not only the new Bellanca plane but also the services of its talented designer, Giuseppe Bellanca, offered to sell his plane to the St. Louis group. The Bellanca was the plane that Lindbergh wanted above all others, believing it to be the best suited for a transatlantic flight. The sale fell through, though, when Levine, unpredictable as ever, said he must retain approval of who would actually fly the plane on the New York-Paris attempt. Lindbergh might not even be chosen to fly his own plane!

Lindbergh, indignant, went to San Diego where, with Ryan's chief engineer, Donald Hall, he began design work on a single-engined monoplane, an adaptation of Ryan's successful M-2 Brougham. Lindbergh was impressed with Hall's competence and the friendly honesty of Ryan's president, B. F. Mahoney. He liked, also, the enthusiasm with which Ryan employees tackled the job. He hoped to take off for Paris by early June. Since it was March and the competing planes were already making flight tests, his chances for the Orteig prize still looked hopeless, or at best remote. Then the uncertainties of early aviation changed the picture.

On April 16, Anthony Fokker, designer, took Byrd's new Fokker trimotor, the *America*, up for a short test flight at Hasbrouck Heights, New Jersey. Aboard, besides Fokker, were three members of the proposed four-man crew for the ocean flight—Floyd Bennett, pilot; George Noville, radio operator; and Byrd. The ship proved to be nose-heavy, probably because the main fuel tank in the fuselage was empty, not being needed for the 40-minute flight. Upon landing, the big plane's tail rose higher and higher until the craft nosed over on its back, injuring Bennett, Byrd, and Noville and putting the *America* in the repair shop for a month. Bennett's injuries put him completely out of the flight.

Ten days later, at Langley Field, Virginia, the *American Legion*, fully loaded to 17,000 pounds for the first time, took off but was unable to gain altitude. Veering to the right to avoid a row of trees, the huge biplane lost flying speed, splashed into a swampy pond and buried its nose in the far bank. Davis and Wooster died in the crash, trapped in the cockpit which was crushed by the nose engine and submerged in the muddy water.

Ironically, two of the three trimotored airplanes, the type generally considered safest for a transoceanic flight, had suffered fatal crashes and were out of the race—first, Fonck's Sikorsky, and now the *American Legion*. The third, Byrd's Fokker, seemed almost out. Suddenly the spotlight shifted to the little single-engined planes—the *Columbia* and the *White Bird*. In San Diego, a continent away from New York, Lindbergh was watching his plane take shape. The young flier, with his boyish good looks, was starting to attract some publicity, but remained a minor character in the drama unfolding.

Lindbergh's chances improved slightly on April 24, shortly after the *Columbia* was officially christened before crowds at Curtiss Field, Long Island. A landing gear attachment failed on

Three competitors: Charles A. Lindbergh, Commander Richard E. Byrd, and Clarence Chamberlin in May, 1927, before their respective transatlantic flights.

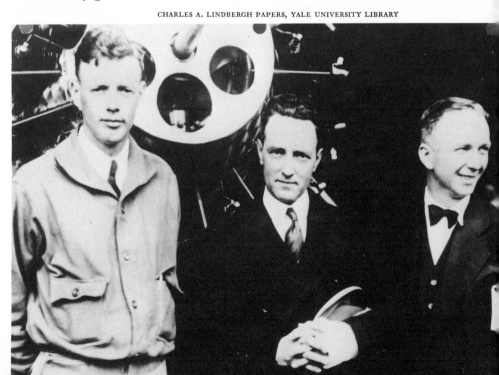

takeoff and the ship was damaged in the ensuing one-wheel landing. Chamberlain set the plane down neatly enough to avert injury to himself and three passengers (including Levine's teenage daughter), but the *Columbia* was grounded for a few days. More serious for the *Columbia* were Levine's doubts and continuing discovery of new reasons to delay the takeoff for Paris. On April 30, for example, he revealed that three new radios had been ordered and would have to be tested individually before he could decide which one should be installed for the big flight.

Meanwhile, in France, Nungesser and Coli were awaiting good weather and hoping for a tailwind at least part of the way—a slim hope on an east-west crossing. The French newspapers taunted them, mocking their "timidity." Finally, in the predawn gray of May 8, the *White Bird* made its hazardous takeoff across the grass of Le Bourget Field, staggering into the air after a run of about a mile. The first plane to get airborne for the Orteig prize, the fuel-heavy ship droned low across the French countryside, Nungesser dropping the landing gear as he struggled for altitude. Accompanying planes watched as Nungesser and Coli reached the coast 90 minutes after takeoff and headed bravely out over the ocean. Except for a later sighting off the Irish coast, they were never seen again. What brought them down—storms, ice, headwinds, engine failure, a flying mistake, navigational errors? Any one would have been enough. The *White Bird* may even have crossed the ocean and crashed in the trackless wilds of Newfoundland. The answer will probably never be known.

Now the field was reduced to the *Columbia*, still beset by bickerings and legal actions; the *America*, her crash damage almost completely repaired; and, in San Diego, the Lindbergh plane, now named the *Spirit of St. Louis*, built and flight tested in the short span of two months.

Although based on the design of an earlier Ryan monoplane, the *Spirit of St. Louis* had major modifications to make it a long-

The Spirit of St. Louis *takes off from San Diego, on May 10, 1927, for St. Louis and New York and its rendezvous with history.*

range plane. Since Lindbergh wanted to fly alone, without a copilot-navigator or even a radio, the weight savings were converted into extra fuel tanks. The plane was designed to carry 425 gallons of gasoline, enough for a 4,100-mile flight (some 500 miles beyond Paris). To lift that load, designer Hall added ten feet to the wing, for a total span of 46 feet. Then he added a stronger landing gear to withstand the dead weight of the fuel load during takeoff.

To improve cruising speed Hall reduced aerodynamic drag. He moved the pilot's cabin from the customary place high and forward to a spot almost halfway back in the fuselage, just under the rear portion of the wing. This eliminated a windshield. All struts were carefully streamlined; even the wheels were covered with a tight fabric fairing. These efforts added perhaps ten miles an hour to the plane's speed, a vital gain for the long flight ahead. For better balance, the main fuel tank was set just ahead of the pilot's cockpit, at the plane's center of gravity. This made the *Spirit of St. Louis* a "blind" ship, since Lindbergh could not see straight ahead. However, two open side windows, along with a small periscope for use when necessary, gave him sufficient forward visibility for safe flight.

The Spirit of St. Louis *was based on the design of an earlier Ryan monoplane but had major changes for the transatlantic attempt.*

The most dependable and popular power combination of the time, a 220-horsepower Wright J-5 Whirlwind engine and a two-bladed Standard Steel propeller, pulled the *Spirit of St. Louis* along at a cruising speed of 100 miles an hour. (Its top speed, with a light fuel load, was about 130 miles an hour.) The Whirlwind, a 9-cylinder, air-cooled, radial engine, also powered the *Columbia, America,* and *American Legion.*

As work on the *Spirit of St. Louis* was rushed to completion, with all other work at Ryan suspended, Lindbergh mapped out his transatlantic route. Since he expected to cover 100 miles for each hour of flight, he plotted his course in 100-mile segments. He chose to navigate by dead reckoning, carrying no sextant, and taking his chances on drifting off course. It would be difficult, he reasoned, to miss anything as large as the continent of Europe!

On April 28, Lindbergh took the *Spirit of St. Louis* up on its first flight and in the days that followed flew a series of performance and weight tests. He made a 28-second takeoff run with a 300-gallon fuel load, the heaviest he dared to attempt during the test stage.

On the afternoon of May 10 Lindbergh took off for St. Louis, his plane carrying about half the fuel load it would have to lift on the takeoff for Paris. Crossing the Rockies and the Great Plains at night, he landed at Lambert Field, St. Louis, at 6:20 A.M., 14 hours and 25 minutes after leaving San Diego, a record for that time. Fortunately, he learned on the flight that the Whirlwind needed a carburetor heater, for the engine coughed and almost quit at the higher altitudes over the mountains. The heater was installed in time for the ocean flight.

On the next morning (May 12) Lindbergh took off for New York, landing at Curtiss Field in 7 hours and 20 minutes, another record. Clearly the newcomer had become not only a serious contender, but also the most newsworthy in view of his dramatic cross-country dash and the fact that he was going to fly alone. Even though Byrd's Fokker, its repairs completed, arrived at Roosevelt Field the same day, reporters and cameramen zeroed in on Lindbergh. He was on his way to headline and newsreel fame as the "Lone Eagle" and the "Flying Fool."

Lindbergh chose Roosevelt Field for his takeoff, since it had about a mile of runway, longer than either Curtiss or nearby Mitchel. The growing publicity brought crowds to Long Island every day (30,000 mobbed the fields on Sunday, May 14). Despite this and other distractions, Lindbergh completed his preparations. He found that his fuel tanks held 450 gallons instead of the estimated 425, an increase of 150 pounds. To partially offset this he cut his oil supply from 25 to 20 gallons (saving 35 pounds), since the Whirlwind had not burned much oil on the transcontinental flight. At Roosevelt, he paced off the sand and cinder flight strip, noting its narrowness and none-too-smooth surface. One of the more critical decisions to be made was the selection of the plane's propeller pitch setting. The propeller was adjustable only on the ground and the setting, once made, would prevail for the whole flight. Thus the setting had to be a delicate compromise between the low blade angle for a safe takeoff and the high angle for economic cruising (the best gas mileage).

In New York, Lindbergh awaits favorable weather forecast for his New York-Paris flight.

After conferring with the propeller experts, Lindbergh chose a pitch angle of 16.25 degrees, which favored cruising but reduced takeoff performance. That setting, in fact, gave the Whirlwind only 190 of its maximum 220 horsepower. It was a courageous gamble, for the *Spirit of St. Louis* would weigh almost 5,200 pounds at takeoff, far more than it had ever weighed before, and for real takeoff safety needed every bit of power available.

Years later, when asked about the risky choice, Lindbergh said: "We felt edgy about the range. Time was short and we lacked the benefits of a lot of tests. I decided to 'feel' the plane off the ground just as I'd done in underpowered planes while barnstorming. If I felt I was not going to get off the ground, my plan was simply to cut the throttle." In short, he was saying that it wouldn't make sense to get safely off the ground only to run out of fuel before reaching Europe.

His preparations completed, Lindbergh awaited a favorable weather report. The man of the hour, now, was James H. (Doc) Kimball of the U.S Weather Bureau, a leading forecaster. For days he pored over his maps, coordinating information received from Cape Cod to Newfoundland and from ships at sea. On the night of May 19 he found the conditions he wanted—a good chance of clear skies and tailwinds along most of the route.

With only a few hours of sleep, Lindbergh hurried to Curtiss Field in the early morning darkness of May 20. The *Spirit of St. Louis* was fueled (by 4:00 A.M.) and towed through a light rain to the west end of adjoining Roosevelt Field where it was pointed east along the muddy, puddle-spotted strip. Carl F. Schory of the National Aeronautics Association installed the

Charles Lindbergh fastens the belt of his flying suit just before the takeoff for Paris, May 20, 1927, at 7:52 A.M.

CHARLES A. LINDBERGH PAPERS,
YALE UNIVERSITY LIBRARY

official NAA barograph behind the pilot's seat, while Wright's best engine experts gave the Whirlwind a final inspection. At daybreak Lindbergh, clad in a bulky flying suit, squeezed into the tiny cockpit. He waved to his friends and helpers and gunned the engine. Ahead, barely visible through the mist, stood the flight's first obstacle, a row of telephone wires at the far end of the runway.

The story of that takeoff has been told and retold: how the overloaded plane struggled to break free of the mud, moving slowly at first, then gaining speed; how it splashed through the puddles, lifting from the ground at the 2,000-foot mark, but sinking back again, lifting for a second time at 3,000 feet, then once more settling back; up finally at 4,200 feet with only 800 feet remaining; leveling out as Lindbergh held it down to obtain the added speed which meant control, then pulling up to clear the dreaded telephone wires by a scant 20 feet. The time was 7:50 A.M. The "dark horse," by staying alert to Doc Kimball's weather forecasts, and then reacting quickly and decisively, had left the competition at the starting gate.

Flying at only 200 feet, under a heavy overcast, Lindbergh pointed the *Spirit of St. Louis* northeast along the Great Circle route. He passed over Long Island Sound, Rhode Island, and Cape Cod. Then, still flying low, he crossed the 250 miles of open sea to Nova Scotia. A three-hour flight along that scenic peninsula, through rainstorms and rough air, followed by a two-hour over-water hop, brought him to Newfoundland, the last place he could make an emergency landing before heading out over the ocean. With almost no sleep for over 24 hours, he fought to stay awake. He flew over St. John's, already aloft for 11 hours as he passed the place where Alcock and Brown had begun their flight nearly eight years before.

The coast of Newfoundland faded behind him in the dusk, and he faced a lonely and uncertain night, his plane a tiny speck above a hostile sea. He was on course, riding a tailwind, his engine running smoothly and with fuel consumption exactly as planned. At the 12-hour mark he had covered 1,200 miles, one-third of the way to Paris, and precisely on schedule. He was changing his course slightly to the east every 100 miles as he held to the Great Circle route.

The night brought fog and Lindbergh nosed the ship up through the mists, getting "on top" for awhile at 5,000 feet, but later forced up to 10,000 feet with even higher clouds looming ahead. The cold night air helped keep him awake. The little plane bounced in the turbulence as it plunged into a wall of clouds. Ice formed on the struts and wings, adding dangerously to the ship's weight and making response to the controls sluggish and uncertain. Lindbergh dropped down to warmer altitudes and the ice melted and broke free, but again he had to fight to stay awake.

At 1:00 A.M. New York time, the *Spirit of St. Louis* passed the halfway mark (point of no return), flying in scattered clouds at 9,500 feet. Lindbergh's drowsiness became worse. He dozed off intermittently, awaking each time as the unstable plane veered sharply up or down, the roar of its engine changing in pitch and intensity.

Traveling east, the *Spirit of St. Louis* flew into an early dawn and Lindbergh caught a brief glimpse of a bright morning sun before plunging once more into the clouds. Flying by instrument and concerned about the wind direction, he dropped down almost to sea level for a look. The waves showed that he still had a tailwind. He climbed again to a safer altitude as the clouds ahead thickened, reaching almost to the ocean's surface. His constant fight to stay awake had hindered his navigation and he worried about how far he might have drifted off course. He estimated he had about 150 gallons of gasoline left, more than enough to carry him the remaining 1,300 miles to Paris.

The weather cleared as the morning passed. Lindbergh saw a sea gull and a school of porpoise, the first signs of life since he'd

French police tried in vain to keep crowds away from the Spirit of
St. Louis *after Lindbergh's landing at Le Bourget Field.*

left Newfoundland. A fleet of small fishing boats hove into view
and he glided down, his engine throttled, and shouted, "Which
way is Ireland?" No sign came from the astonished fishermen.

Less than an hour later, almost 28 hours aloft, he saw land
ahead. As he crossed the coastline his map showed him he was
over Dingle Bay and the town of Valencia, Ireland, almost exactly on course—a near miracle of navigation. He was well ahead
of schedule, being only 16 hours out of Newfoundland when
he'd allowed himself 18½ hours. The tailwinds had been stronger
than expected. Now, if the clear weather held, the worst was
over.

He flew across southwestern England and the English Channel and, in the setting sun, saw the French coast ahead. Lights
were twinkling on in the city of Cherbourg as he passed overhead and aimed for Deauville at the mouth of the Seine River.
He nibbled at a chicken sandwich but, elated at being so close
to his goal, found himself not hungry despite not having eaten

since before his takeoff. (It was now 4:30 P.M. New York time, 9:30 P.M. in France.)

Paris, the "City of Light," proved easy to find, a glowing expanse in a countryside which was dark in contrast. He circled the floodlit Eiffel Tower before heading northeast to find Le Bourget Field. Soon he saw a large dark area surrounded by a myriad of lights which seemed to converge from all directions. The dark patch was Le Bourget, while the lights were those of hundreds of automobiles, jammed bumper to bumper as thousands drove to the field to hail the flier—and to see history made.

Spotting a lighted windsock, Lindbergh made a cautious pass low over the field, circled again and landed—the first night landing he'd made in the *Spirit of St. Louis*. The official time of landing was 10:22 P.M. Paris time (5:22 P.M. New York time). Lindbergh had been in the air 33 hours, 30 minutes since leaving New York. He shut off the engine as the cheering, almost hysterical, crowds broke through police barriers and surged toward the plane. The epic flight was over, the Orteig prize was his, but Lindbergh's life as a hero had just begun.

Lindbergh was the 67th person to fly the Atlantic nonstop. As we have seen, Alcock and Brown, followed by 31 men aboard

The Columbia *in flight shortly after taking off from New York on its transatlantic flight which ended in Germany.*

LEWIS R. BERLEPSCH COLLECTION

The Columbia *in Germany after its transatlantic flight. The word
"Paris" was painted out before takeoff, since Chamberlin and Levine
intended to fly beyond the French capital.*

the R-34 dirigible, crossed in 1919. The German zeppelin ZR-3
(used later by the U.S Navy as the *Los Angeles*) flew to Lake-
hurst, New Jersey, in 1924 with a crew of 33.

After Lindbergh's flight there were seventeen other attempts
in 1927 to fly the Atlantic. Only two were successful: the *Columbia* flew from New York to Germany on June 4-6, covering a
record 3,911 miles nonstop, with Chamberlin as pilot and
Levine going along as a passenger, climbing aboard at the last
minute to the surprise of everyone. The *America* crossed also, on
June 29-July 1, but was forced by fog to land in the Channel off
the French coast.

The remaining fifteen flights either never got started, or were
cancelled en route (the planes turning back), or ended with
aircraft lost at sea. A total of twelve persons died. The final
attempt, on December 24, resulted in the loss of Mrs. Frances
Grayson's Sikorsky S-36 amphibian, the *Dawn*, during a foolhardy flight in winter weather. Lost with Mrs. Grayson were her
pilot, navigator, and engineer.

Outstanding among the early transatlantic flights were two world distance records. Russell Boardman and John Polando flew their Bellanca, the *Cape Cod*, from New York to Istanbul, Turkey, July 28–30, 1931, a nonstop distance record of 5,011 miles. That mark stood until August 5–7, 1933, when the Frenchmen Paul Codos and Maurice Rossi flew a single-engined Bleriot-Zappata monoplane, the *Joseph LeBrix*, from New York to Rayak, Syria, a distance of 5,657 miles.

In the summer of 1927 Lindbergh toured the United States in the *Spirit of St. Louis* to show the huge crowds that cheered him at every stop that air transportation could be as reliable as the crack trains in that age of rail travel. He flew 22,350 miles, visiting eighty-two cities and covering all of the then forty-eight states. He missed only one scheduled appearance—in Portland,

On tour during the summer of 1927, Lindbergh, shown here in Boston, preached a vision of future air transportation.

YANKEE MAGAZINE, ALTON H. BLACKINGTON COLLECTION

When fog prevented landing at Portland, Maine, during his 22,000-mile tour of the U.S., Lindbergh came down at Concord, New Hampshire.

Maine, because of heavy fog. He preached a clear vision of future air transportation. "The places that have airports will be far ahead of those without them," he predicted.

Why did Lindbergh fly the ocean alone? In addition to the weight saving, it was because, as he said later, he was willing to risk his own life but not someone else's. Independent by nature, he wanted total control of the situation. In later years, as an aviation consultant, he often traveled the world's airways alone,

This scene in Concord was typical as Lindbergh toured the United States in the summer of 1927.

Right: *Final home for the* Spirit of St. Louis *is the National Air and Space Museum, Washington, D.C.*

his "luggage" only a briefcase containing his papers, a clean shirt, socks, toothbrush, and razor.

In the 1930s, as an experimental pilot and explorer, he moved beyond the initial heroism of his New York-Paris flight to help build United States leadership in aviation. Each of his flights had a purpose, usually the improvement of airline planning and technical developments. He selected new routes and recommended new types of aircraft, including the first jetliners. As early as 1933, in a report on future transatlantic air service, he wrote: "I believe that in the future, aircraft will detour bad weather areas by flying above them rather than around them," which is what jet airliners do today.

Lindbergh's independent nature led him to take positions unpopular with the Roosevelt administration and the pro-war groups. In a televised interview in 1977 commentator Eric Severeid asked Anne Morrow Lindbergh, "Why didn't Charles Lindbergh take advice?" (in reference to Lindbergh's pre-war political speeches without taking any advice on them).

Mrs. Lindbergh replied in part: "He never listened to anyone. He listened to himself . . . if he had listened to people, he would never have flown to Paris."

H. H. LIPPINCOTT

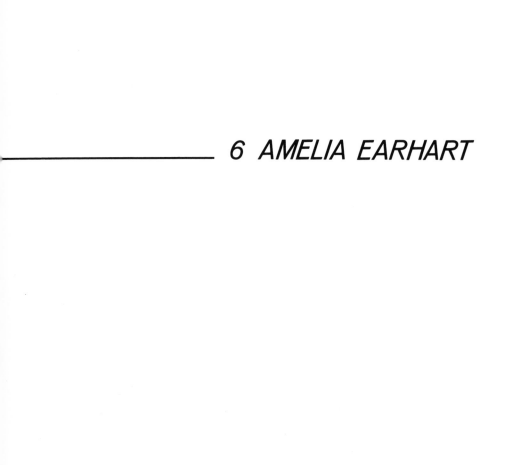

6 AMELIA EARHART

Three More Firsts _____

By 1928 the successful transatlantic flights totaled twelve, among them the "firsts" already described. Yet there remained a milestone unreached—the first air crossing by a woman. Not that the ladies had not been attracted by the idea, for female hopefuls had made three transatlantic attempts in late 1927, all without success and two with tragic results.

First to try was Princess Anne Lowenstein-Wertheim of England who, in her sixties, made the attempt despite desperate efforts by her family to stop her. The princess flew as a passenger in a big single-engined Fokker monoplane, the *St. Raphael*, piloted by two veteran British fliers, Leslie Hamilton and F. F. Minchin. The *St. Raphael* lifted from Upavon Airdrome on the Salisbury Plains, 100 miles west of London, on the dark and misty morning of August 31, 1927, bound for Ottawa, Canada. She was sighted at points over England and Ireland and then, like the *White Bird* before her, was never seen again. Before disappearing she had been averaging only 70 miles an hour ground speed, far slower than the hoped-for 100. It was an ill-advised flight against strong headwinds and into what ship crews later described as "terrible weather" at sea.

On the other side of the ocean, at New York's Roosevelt Field, two more competitors kept a wary eye on each other throughout September. Yearning to make aviation history were two opposites, twenty-three-year-old Ruth Elder, a strikingly beautiful brunette of moderate means, and Mrs. Frances Wilson Grayson, a multimillionaire real estate operator in her mid-thirties.

Miss Elder (actually she was Mrs. Lyle Womack of Lakeland, Florida, a fact she had kept secret to maintain her glamorous image) got away first. The plane, a single-engined Stinson Detroiter monoplane, the *American Girl*, bought with the help of Florida and West Virginia businessmen, left New York in the late afternoon of October 11. The pilot, George Haldeman, an airplane salesman who was also Miss Elder's flight instructor, headed the Wright Whirlwind-powered craft due east over the warmer, but longer, southern route. It was late in the season and this heading would avoid the icing conditions along the Great Circle route to the north. Also it would put them closer to the shipping lanes.

It was a wise choice. After a flight of 2,600 miles, which included a bumpy and terrifying night in a rainstorm, the *American Girl* was forced into the sea by a broken oil line. The plane splashed into the water near a Dutch tanker whose crew rescued the fliers. They were 500 miles west of Portugal, well short of their goal, Paris.

Meanwhile Mrs. Grayson's hopes for a transatlantic crossing in her Sikorsky amphibian, the *Dawn*, were beset by mechanical troubles, three unsuccessful starts, and finally by doubts as to the plane's ability to carry enough fuel for the crossing. These misadventures occurred at Old Orchard Beach, Maine, the takeoff point, and the *Dawn* was returned to New York at the end of October for further tests. Pilot Wilmer (Bill) Stultz, disliking the look of things, resigned and was replaced by Oscar Omdahl. Ignoring widespread warnings against an ocean flight in the winter, Mrs. Grayson left Roosevelt Field on Christmas Eve for Harbour Grace, Newfoundland, her new takeoff point. Aboard the *Dawn*, besides the owner, were Omdahl as pilot, Bryce Goldsborough, navigator, and Fred Schroeder, mechanic. They were never seen again. The Atlantic, its murderous winter weather sadly underestimated, had claimed four more victims.

Early in 1928 a fourth and equally unsuccessful attempt by a woman occurred. Elsie Mackay, a pilot, ex-actress, and daughter of a British shipowner, Lord Inchcape, teamed up with Walter Hinchcliffe, an Imperial Airways pilot. The two Britons took off from England on March 13 in a Stinson Detroiter, the *Endeavor*. They, too, were never seen again. Disaster had struck early in the flight, for parts of the plane washed ashore on the northwest coast of Ireland.

Despite these setbacks, the quest continued. In the United States two more competitors were making headlines. Mabel (Mibs) Boll, an heiress whom the press dubbed "the Queen of Diamonds," was offering $25,000 to a pilot to fly her across, but had found no takers. Mrs. Frederick Guest, wife of a British aviation leader, proposed to fly as a passenger in a pontoon-fitted Fokker trimotor, the *Friendship*, purchased from Commander Byrd. (Byrd had accepted a Ford trimotor from Henry Ford and did not need the Fokker for his projected flight over the South Pole.)

Mrs. Guest, at the insistence of her family, bowed out and her place was taken by twenty-nine-year-old Amelia Earhart, a teacher in a settlement house in Boston. Miss Earhart, a pilot with 500 flight hours (none of which was instrument flying) bore a striking resemblance to Lindbergh. She was also an independent, tough-minded person of intelligence and sensitivity. George Palmer Putnam, a book publisher, and Hilton H. Railey, a skilled public relations man, who had been commissioned to select Mrs. Guest's replacement, recognized quickly that they had found the right person. They kept their find a secret to avoid the publicity which would both alert competitors and interfere with preparations for the flight.

Still in secrecy, the *Friendship* left Boston for Trepassey, Newfoundland, the morning of June 3 with Bill Stultz, pilot; Louis (Slim) Gordon, mechanic; and Miss Earhart as a passenger. Fog forced them down at Halifax, Nova Scotia, but they flew on to Trepassey the next day.

Miss Earhart's presence aboard was discovered during the unscheduled stop at Halifax, a discovery which dismayed Mibs Boll. Stultz, she said, had promised to fly *her* to Europe in the *Columbia*, which she had obtained on loan from Charles Levine! Quickly, she hired Oliver LeBoutillier, pilot, and Arthur Argles, navigator, and the trio flew in the *Columbia* to Harbour Grace, Newfoundland, 60 miles north of Trepassey. The two women and their crews waited for the weather to lift.

The wait covered fifteen days. The Trepassey skies cleared first and on June 17, after three unsuccessful attempts, the fuel-laden *Friendship* struggled from the waters of the bay and headed east. By the time the weather cleared at Harbour Grace the luckless Miss Boll had lost her chance to be first. The *Columbia* returned to New York.

As the big red and orange seaplane flew through a cloudy night the flying burden fell on Stultz who, at twenty-seven, was already a veteran pilot with Army, Navy, and commercial experience. As usual on ocean flights of the time, trouble struck early. The radio went dead which, with the clouds and fog, made it difficult to determine the plane's position and direction. Flying blind, Stultz relied on his instruments for almost the entire flight.

Friendship, the trimotor Fokker seaplane in which Amelia Earhart became the first woman to cross the Atlantic by air.

Meanwhile, Miss Earhart (or AE, as her associates called her) knelt wedged between fuel tanks at a low table near a window, keeping a running and often lyrical log of the flight. Of the view before nightfall she wrote: "Marvelous shapes in white stand out, some trailing shimmering veils. The clouds look like icebergs . . . The highest peaks of the fog mountains are tinted pink with the setting sun. The hollows are gray and shadowy . . . I am getting housemaid's knee kneeling here at the table gulping beauty."

At daybreak Stultz brought the *Friendship* down through the clouds close to the sea, sensing that with no radio they were probably off course. They spotted a ship and noticed that their course was not parallel to that of the vessel. (The ship was the liner, *America*, they learned later.) They dropped two messages, each tied to an orange, but both missed and fell into the sea. They were asking for some sign from the ship as to their correct course eastward. They considered landing near the ship, but the waves looked too high. It would be safer, they decided, to fly on, even though they had only an hour's fuel left. Although they did not know it, they were over the Irish Sea a mere 70 miles from the English coast. Invisible in the fog, Ireland already lay well astern.

Dropping low beneath the clouds, they crossed the coastline and Stultz set the *Friendship* down in a bay off the small factory town of Burry Port in Wales, 20 hours, 40 minutes after lifting from the water at Trepassey. The first woman to cross the Atlantic by air had made it without once touching the controls, which was only right since her flight experience at the time consisted only of fair weather flying in small planes.

Uneasy in the spotlight of fame and publicity, Miss Earhart insisted that all credit should go to Stultz. Replying to a message of congratulations from President Coolidge, she wired: "Success entirely due great skill of Mr. Stultz. He was only one mile off course at Valentia after flying blind for 2,246 miles at average speed of 113 m.p.h."

When she returned to the United States, Miss Earhart, like Lindbergh the year before, decided to promote aviation. She crisscrossed the country in a little Avian biplane bought from Lady Heath, one of England's leading female fliers. She lectured, wrote, and set several air records, always stressing that women could do well in any field, especially aviation. In 1931 she married Mr. Putnam, who had become her business manager, but retained her independent career and identity as Amelia Earhart, rarely being referred to as "Mrs. Putnam." Her husband was the first to admit that nobody ever "managed" Amelia Earhart.

For Amelia Earhart the flight in the *Friendship* had left much to be desired in terms of personal achievement. True, it had brought her fame and a whole new life. Yet she knew she had contributed little to the flight and, in her own words, had been no more than "a sack of potatoes" aboard. She dreamed of really flying the Atlantic—as the pilot—and she wanted to do it alone.

Those were the "firsts" she had in mind when, at breakfast in late 1931, she quietly asked her husband: "Would you mind if I flew the Atlantic?"

In the three-and-a-half years since the *Friendship*'s flight Miss Earhart had taken time from the demands of public appearances to log about a thousand more flight hours, using many of them to learn instrument flying. She felt she was ready to challenge the ocean on her own, but wanted to make sure. In April, 1932, she conferred with Bernt Balchen, the great Norwegian-born flier, a veteran of Atlantic and Antarctic flights with Byrd, and asked him three questions: Was she ready? Was the plane ready? Would he help? Balchen stood silent for a while, then answered "yes" to all three.

The plane was a Lockheed Vega, a full cantilever craft, its single, tapered wing devoid of all external bracing, probably the

At Teterboro Airport, New Jersey, Amelia Earhart stands before her Lockheed Vega with Eddie Gorski (left), her mechanic, and Bernt Balchen, her technical advisor, in May, 1932.

UNITED TECHNOLOGIES CORPORATION

sleekest, most efficient aircraft of its day. Miss Earhart had been flying it for more than two years and it needed changes for the Atlantic flight. At Teterboro, New Jersey, Airport, and under Balchen's direction, the fuselage was strengthened, more fuel tanks inserted, a drift indicator and three compasses added, and a new 450-horsepower Pratt & Whitney Wasp engine installed.

As she prepared for the flight, Miss Earhart knew that two more women had tried, and failed, to fly the Atlantic the year before. On January 7, 1931, Beryl Hart, holder of a transport pilot's license, with William S. MacLaren as copilot-navigator, took off from Hampton Roads, Virginia, in the Bellanca *Tradewind*, but disappeared between Bermuda and the Azores. On June 22, Ruth Nichols, in a solo attempt, cracked up her Lockheed Vega in a landing at St. John, New Brunswick, suffering back injuries which removed her from the competition. Two other leading American pilots, Elinor Smith and Laura Ingalls, were also considering Atlantic flights.

In May, all preparations completed, AE and her aides awaited favorable weather, with meteorolgist Doc Kimball once more the key figure. On May 18 Kimball predicted clear skies between New York and Harbour Grace, Miss Earhart's proposed takeoff point, and reasonably good conditions from there to England. The Vega left Teterboro the next day for St. John, remained there overnight and reached Harbour Grace the following afternoon. Balchen did the flying while AE stretched out aft of the fuselage fuel tank, resting up for the solo test ahead. Also aboard was mechanic Eddie Gorski.

This time there were no long days of waiting in Newfoundland. Both plane and pilot were ready and the weather, while not perfect, was at least promising. It was time to go. After a short nap, Miss Earhart, clad in a leather flying suit and carrying a helmet and mittens, strode to the waiting Vega.

"OK. So long. Good luck," said Balchen, who never wasted words. A quick handshake with Balchen and Gorski, and AE

Amelia Earhart enters cockpit of her Lockheed Vega prior to her solo flight across the Atlantic, May 20–21, 1932.

climbed up into the cockpit just forward of the wing. Within minutes she gunned the Vega down the airstrip to a smooth takeoff. The time: 7:12 P.M. The date: May 20, just five years to the day since Lindbergh had started *his* solo flight.

With the setting sun at her back she climbed through clear skies to 12,000 feet, enjoying the view along with the smooth air. All was well, almost too well. Was this to be, finally, an ocean flight without trouble? For several hours, yes, but then a freak malfunction occurred: the altimeter failed, a misfortune she'd never met in her twelve years of flying. She watched the dials spin aimlessly and knew this vital instrument was "out" for the duration of the flight. It was a "first" she had not expected.

In fair weather a failed altimeter usually presents no major problem. But in the black of night—about 11:30 P.M.—and with

clouds closing in, it made for a more serious situation. The Vega
began to pitch and toss in the turbulent air. Lightning flashed
about and AE could only guess her height above the sea.

An hour later the clouds parted for a few moments and the
moon shone briefly. Miss Earhart pointed the Vega's nose up-
ward to stay clear of other storms that might lie ahead.

She climbed for a half hour, then noticed ice forming on the
wings. The controls became sluggish and the Vega wallowed
through the air. Then, like the Vimy thirteen years before, it
stalled and fell into a spin. With no altimeter, and in the pitch
black of a stormy night, Miss Earhart's peril could hardly have
been worse. As she plunged toward the sea she did what should
be done to right a spinning plane—put the controls in neutral.
At lower altitude the ice began to melt, the spin stopped, and
the Vega flew level again. Below, "too close for comfort," as she
wrote later, and despite the darkness, Miss Earhart could see the
whitecaps breaking.

Later, the barograph, an instrument that records a plane's

*The plane in which Amelia Earhart made her solo flight across the
Atlantic is in the National Air and Space Museum, Washington, D.C.*

ascent and descent, confirmed the Vega's near-fatal plunge toward the sea: it had registered an almost vertical drop of 3,000 feet.

More danger arrived and persisted for the rest of the flight. Flames suddenly trailed from a broken weld in the engine's exhaust collector ring—a disturbing sight at any time but terrifying in its brilliant glow at night. For a moment AE thought of turning back, but knew she could not make a safe landing in the still fuel-heavy plane, even if she were lucky enough to find the airstrip at Harbour Grace. She flew on, the broken weld apparently not getting worse, and with daybreak the flames at least looked less threatening.

After 10 hours aloft, five of them in the storm, Miss Earhart guessed that a northwest wind had forced her off course to the south. She turned northeast to make sure she did not miss the southern tip of Ireland. Soon, nearing the final hour of her flight, she peered hopefully ahead for land. "The last hour of an ocean flight is the hardest," she wrote later. "You constantly see mirages of land in the clouds that fade away nearly as fast as they appear. You feel you are near land—and imagination seems to do the rest."

Shortly afterward she crossed the coastline of Ireland. Clouds and thunderstorms blanketed the unfamiliar hills ahead, a danger to be avoided, especially with no altimeter. She swung north and followed a railroad. A village appeared, with green pastures stretching for miles about. Selecting a gently sloping field, which seemed to have the fewest cows, she set the Vega down to a smooth landing as the bovines scattered.

A small crowd gathered and she learned she was on the farm of Patrick Gallagher in the little town of Culmore, some six miles from Londonderry, Ireland. The flight had taken 14 hours, 56 minutes and, upon its completion, Amelia Earhart's Atlantic "firsts" included: first woman to cross the Atlantic by air; first woman to pilot a plane across; and first woman to make a solo flight across. She had the added distinctions of being the second person to fly the Atlantic alone, the only person to cross twice by air, the pilot of the fastest transatlantic flight up to that time, and the holder of a new distance record for women pilots.

Returning to the United States as the most famous woman flier in the world, Miss Earhart resumed her work for the twin causes of aviation and women. She wrote two books, plus poetry and magazine articles. She taught at Purdue University as Counselor for Careers for Women. She was in demand as a lecturer. She set more air records, including a Pacific solo from Hawaii to California. Through it all she continued to live life, as she put it, "for the fun of it." This led to what she intended to be the final long-distance flying of her career, a round-the-world trip, which ended with her tragic and mysterious disappearance in the Pacific.

The trip was made in a new twin-engined Lockheed Electra, a flying laboratory paid for by the Purdue-inspired Amelia Earhart Fund for Aeronautical Research. After circling the globe, Miss Earhart and her navigator, Frederick Noonan, had only the Pacific crossing left to complete their journey.

The first leg of that crossing was the riskiest—a 2,500-mile over-water hop from Lae, New Guinea, to a tiny dot in the ocean called Howland Island. It was a tough target to hit even in the best of weather, and conditions the night of July 2, 1937, were far from perfect. Turbulence and a high overcast interfered with Noonan's navigation. For most of the flight he saw neither the sun nor the stars.

They never reached Howland, although radio flashes from the Electra showed that they had approached close to the island. Lost and with their fuel gone, what happened to them? Most believed they had ditched and been lost at sea. But with the passage of years, doubts arose. Rumors grew that they had been captured after crash-landing on a Japanese-occupied island. Later investigations seemed to strengthen that theory. Fred

Goerner, a TV reporter, spearheaded a six-year (1960–66) study of the mystery, making four trips into the Pacific and interviewing thousands. He concluded that the Electra, early in its flight, had veered north of its course to observe secret Japanese military installations on the island of Truk, doing so with the full knowledge of some United States military and government officials. Miss Earhart, his studies indicated, had died in captivity, probably of dysentery, while Noonan had been executed. Their government, Goerner concluded, was powerless to help them, fearing that such action would lead to a war for which the United States was not prepared.

So the mystery remains.

Amelia Earhart never underrated the risks of ocean flying. Before her first transatlantic crossing she left two letters to be opened if she were lost. To her father she wrote, "I wish I had won, but it was worthwhile anyway. . . ." For her mother, she left this thought: "My life really has been very happy, and I didn't mind contemplating its end in the midst of it."

7 THE BREMEN AND THE

QUESTION MARK
More East-West Firsts _____

THE FIRST THREE famous first flights across the Atlantic from Europe to the American continent bear striking similarities to their counterpart flights achieved earlier from America to Europe.

The initial crossings were completed, as we have seen, by the U.S. Navy's big NC-4 flying boat, west to east, in 1919, and by the U.S. Army's two World Cruisers, east to west, in 1924. Both were relatively slow flights requiring scheduled stops en route, and both were made by military aircraft supported by service equipment and personnel along the way.

Also similar were the first nonstop flights—the Vimy west to east in 1919 from Newfoundland to Ireland, and the *Bremen* (which we will describe in this chapter) in 1928 from Ireland to Labrador. Both were civilian-owned aircraft flown over roughly comparable routes and distances. Finally, Lindbergh's nonstop hop over the New York-Paris route in a civilian aircraft designed especially for the flight was successfully reversed in 1930 by a French-built civilian airplane, the *Question Mark*, also specifically developed for long-distance flying.

Despite such similarities, however, the east-west crossings of 1928 and 1930, like all the early transatlantic attempts, were marked by their own unique problems, hazards, and achievements. First, the *Bremen*:

The two Germans and the Irishman who formed the crew of the *Bremen* were among the luckiest ever to survive an Atlantic crossing. Baron Gunther von Huenfeld, Hermann Koehl (pilot), and Captain James C. Fitzmaurice of the Irish Free State Army Air Corps flew bravely in the face of the usual odds against a successful east-west flight. Five of their predecessors, the year

Technicians at work on the Bremen *before its east-west crossing of the Atlantic. Insets show crew, left to right, Baron Gunther von Huenfeld, Captain James Fitzmaurice, and Hermann Koehl.*

NATIONAL AIR AND SPACE MUSEUM, SMITHSONIAN INSTITUTION

before, had died in the attempt—Nungesser and Coli in the *White Bird*, and Minchin, Hamilton, and Princess Lowenstein-Wertheim aboard the *St. Raphael*. The *Bremen* itself had failed the previous year, although its crew had lived to tell the tale.

On August 14, 1927, the *Bremen* and its twin Junkers W-33L monoplane, the *Europa*, had taken off from the Junkers plant in Dessau, Germany, on a hoped-for nonstop transatlantic flight. Engine trouble forced the *Europa* to return and the *Bremen* continued alone, flying as far as southern Ireland before being turned back by headwinds and dense clouds. After a meandering flight of 1,800 miles and 22 hours, the *Bremen* was back again on the ground at Dessau, its crew sadder but wiser. Koehl, von Huenfeld, and a third German, Friedrich Loose, had gained a first-hand knowledge of the difficulties involved in trying to fly the Atlantic from east to west.

From this experience, von Huenfeld and Koehl decided to shorten the route by taking off from Ireland on their next attempt. They selected Baldonnel Aerodrome near Dublin as their takeoff point and flew the *Bremen* there from Dessau on March 26, 1928. With them was a copilot, Arthur Spindler, but they sent him back to Germany, replacing him with Fitzmaurice, a pilot of many years experience and a veteran of an unsuccessful transatlantic attempt in September, 1927.

The *Bremen*'s earlier attempt had been sponsored by the North German-Lloyd Steamship Lines of which von Huenfeld was publicity manager. The Baron personally financed the new attempt in which he would again fly as a passenger-navigator. Koehl, meanwhile, was dismissed from his job as night flight manager of Lufthansa, the German airline, in the belief that another transatlantic attempt would prove as foolhardy as the *Bremen*'s previous venture.

The *Bremen* was the first really modern airplane to attempt an Atlantic crossing, being built entirely of metal, with a low wing of fully cantilever construction, and an enclosed cabin for

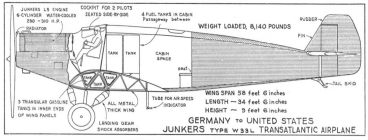

Cutaway drawing shows features of Junkers W33L Bremen, *including closed-type cabin and location of fuel tanks in wings and fuselage.*

the crew. Although its basic design was even then nine years old, the *Bremen*, in 1928, was years ahead of its time. Indeed, it would not look much out of date even today. Its six-cylinder, water-cooled engine developed 310 horsepower. Adapted by Junkers from a wartime B.M.W. engine, it was a reliable, economical power plant.

Yet despite these design advances, the *Bremen* was still an unsatisfactory plane for an Atlantic flight against the west winds. With only moderate power in its single engine and carrying the overload of fuel required for the flight, the *Bremen*'s normal cruise speed of almost 120 miles an hour declined to about 100. To save weight, the craft carried no radio and its safety factor was probably no better than those of other planes which had tried and failed to cross the Atlantic. The *Bremen*'s performance problems quickly showed up as the ship began its takeoff run at Baldonnel at 5:30 A.M. Thursday, April 12, 1928.

Two ambulances had no trouble keeping pace with the *Bremen* as it bumped across the turf field, struggling to attain the 75 miles an hour needed for takeoff. Koehl lifted the *Bremen* clear only a few feet from the end of the field, the plane's landing gear parting the tops of trees. Unable to gain altitude, and with a mountain dead ahead, Koehl had to risk a hazardous turn toward some flat land and a valley behind the plane. A wingtip scraped the grass and brushed through a hedge, but by some

The Junkers monoplane, Bremen, *at Baldonnel Aerodrome near Dublin.*

miracle the overloaded *Bremen* remained airborne. Soon they reached a safe height of 500 feet.

Last sighted over the coastal town of Clifden (where Alcock and Brown had landed nine years before), the *Bremen* headed out over the ocean, starting on the Great Circle course which, its crew hoped, would take them over Newfoundland, Nova Scotia, and then to a safe landing at Mitchel Field, New York. All day the flight proved uneventful, the plane flying through generally clear weather only 100 feet above a calm sea. Koehl and Fitzmaurice alternated at the controls every three hours, while von

The Bremen *in flight during preparations for the Atlantic crossing.*

Huenfeld fixed their position with the sun and dropped smoke bombs every four hours to check for drift.

Nightfall brought their first trouble: the cabin lights failed and after that they had only a flashlight to illuminate their instrument panel. Almost immediately afterward a fuel line broke, filling the cabin with deadly gasoline fumes. Fortunately the broken line was within easy reach, so that it was quickly repaired with tape, and disaster averted.

Throughout the night von Huenfeld sighted the stars to keep them on course but the lack of proper instrument lights made the pilot's job difficult. Headwinds were taking their toll, too, and the *Bremen*'s average speed fell below 60 miles an hour. Even more serious trouble arrived in the early hours of Friday morning: some 400 miles from the American continent they reached the fringes of the Newfoundland fog banks. Soon they could see neither ocean nor sky.

The air became rough as Koehl dropped the *Bremen* close to the sea. The spray of waves beat through the ship's half-open window. "The *Bremen* shook in all its joints," Koehl said later. "The wings were bending and the steering wheel received blow after blow of unusual violence." The compass ran wild, adding to their problems. Climbing again, they plunged on through the clouds, knowing they were near the continent and hoping for a sight of land. Aloft for almost two days, they began to worry about their fuel supply.

They did not know that they had already reached land and, because of a steady drift northward, were now far off course. Unknowingly, they had skirted the whole northeastern coast of Newfoundland and when, in midafternoon of Friday the 13th, they caught their first sight of land it was the icebound coast of Labrador that appeared below them, barely visible through a snow blizzard.

Following the Straits of Belle Isle (which they thought was a river), they sighted a small island covered with snow and ice,

The Bremen *is repaired after its crash landing on Labrador's bleak Greenly Island.*

with what appeared to be a ship frozen against the shore. The "ship" turned out to be a lighthouse on Greenly Island. With the fuel almost gone, Koehl pancaked the *Bremen* as gently as he could onto the frozen surface of a pond, but jagged pieces of ice ripped away the landing gear and damaged the propeller. The fliers stepped out uninjured, to be greeted by the island's total population of fourteen. Soon the world learned through a telegraph station 20 miles away at Point Amour that the *Bremen* was down and its crew safe.

Koehl, von Huenfeld, and Fitzmaurice had flown 2,125 miles in 36 hours, 30 minutes, another Atlantic first, but hardly a triumph of airmanship. For the *Bremen* lay damaged, 1,000 miles from its intended destination, and only by good luck in a spot where help was at hand. Fitzmaurice was flown out in a ski-equipped Canadian "bush" plane, while von Huenfeld and Koehl stayed behind in hopes of repairing the *Bremen* and continuing the flight to New York. Spare parts were flown in and repairs made but the *Bremen*, in an attempted takeoff, was damaged again. Bernt Balchen later flew von Huenfeld and Koehl to New York in Byrd's Ford trimotor which had been fitted with skis for a planned flight over the South Pole.

The three ocean fliers received the usual welcome and honors in New York and Washington as well as in their home countries. The *Bremen* found its final home at the Ford Museum, Dearborn, Michigan.

The best in aircraft design, construction, and flying skills marked the 1930 flight of the French Breguet sesquiplane, *Point d'Interrogation* (the *Question Mark*), from Paris to New York. No pilot of the transatlantic decade was better qualified for this historic flight than Captain Dieudonne Costes nor was any airplane of the time better suited for long-distance flying than this craft which bore the Breguet designation XIX Super T.R. For the first time a transatlantic flight was made to look almost easy, even against the headwinds and over the long Paris-New York route.

A pilot before the first World War, Dieudonne Costes was an "ace" with four years of air combat. When peace came the former fighter pilot joined the French Air Union as one of the first airline pilots flying the Paris-London route. Between late 1926 and 1930, as chief pilot of Breguet, then a leading French manufacturer, he set a series of records for long-distance flying which brought him world renown.

The Breguet XIX Super T.R. was a large single-engined craft with an upper wingspan of almost 60 feet, a narrow lower wing 37 feet long, and a fuselage length of 35 feet. It was the ultimate development from earlier Breguet planes which themselves had evolved from a Breguet general purpose military aircraft.

Several improvements based on the earlier record flights helped make the *Question Mark* the leading long-distance plane of its day. Included were: increasing the fuel capacity from 865 to 1,225 gallons (housed in the fuselage, upper wings, and in two

MUSÉE DE L'AIR, PARIS

Record-breaking Breguet XIX T.R., the Question Mark, *in which Costes and Bellonte made several historic flights.*

"overload" tanks under the lower wing); lengthening the wings and fuselage to handle the extra fuel; increasing the thrust of the Hispano-Suiza engine from 600 to 650 horsepower; widening the gap between the upper and lower wings to give a smooth flow of air over the wings; installing carburetor heaters; and refining the design of the wingtips, ailerons, and tail section.

The distance flights of the *Question Mark* and its predecessor,

The Question Mark's *predecessor, the Breguet XIX G.R. named the* Nungesser-Coli, *was flown by Costes and Joseph LeBrix on a world tour in 1927–28.*

MUSÉE DE L'AIR, PARIS

a Breguet XIX G.R. named the *Nungesser-Coli*, proved the prowess of these fine aircraft, providing a hint of the historic achievement which lay ahead. Here, in brief, are the exploits of the two Breguet planes:

• Paris to Omsk, Siberia, 2,931 miles, (new world distance record). Gilier and Dordilly in a Breguet XIX G.R., July, 1926.

• Paris to Aswan, Egypt, 2,548 miles. Costes and deVitrolles in the XLX G.R., September, 1926.

• Paris to Djask, Persia, 3,387 miles (new world distance record). Costes and Captain Rignot in the XIX G.R., October, 1926.

• Paris to Nijnitagilsk, Siberia, 2,884 miles. Costes and Rignot in the XIX G.R., June, 1927.

• World tour by Costes and Joseph LeBrix in the XIX G.R., now named the *Nungesser-Coli*, Paris to Senegal, Africa. Senegal to Natal, Brazil, 2,125 miles (first nonstop air crossing of the South Atlantic), October, 1927. Flying tour of South and North America with stops at capitals and other major cities. San Francisco to Tokyo by sea, and then by air to Paris, arriving April 14, 1928. Totals: 35,000 miles covered in 338 flying hours.

• Paris to Moulart, Manchuria, 4,913 miles in 51 hours, 19 minutes (new world distance record). Costes and Maurice Bellonte in the Breguet Super T.R., the *Question Mark*, September 27–29, 1929.

• Flight over a closed course in France, 4,990 miles in 53 hours (new world distance record in a closed circuit). Costes and Paul Codos in the Breguet Super T.R., the *Question Mark*, December 15–17, 1929.

• Three records (speed, distance, and duration with a 500-kilogram load), January, 1930, and two records (distance and duration with a 1,000-kilogram load), February, 1930. All by Costes and Codos in the *Question Mark*.

Costes and Bellonte also logged one more valuable experience. On July 13, 1929, they had made an unsuccessful attempt

Dieudonne Costes, left, and his navigator, Maurice Bellonte, first to fly the Atlantic from Paris to New York.

at a Paris-New York flight over the North Atlantic's southern route by way of the Azores. Bad weather, a fuel consumption rate that looked too high, and a broken radio aerial convinced Costes wisely to turn back, and the *Question Mark* landed at Le Bourget Field after a 14-hour flight of 1,600 miles. Costes and François Coty, the millionaire perfume manufacturer who was the *Question Mark*'s chief sponsor, decided to bide their time, improve the plane, and take a more careful look at the weather on the next attempt. Also there seemed to be no serious competition for the Paris-New York flight.

Thus it was that the *Question Mark*, with the design changes noted earlier, stood poised at Le Bourget in late summer of 1930 for its second attempt at a Paris-New York hop. Costes again chose as his partner Bellonte, a mechanic who had also made a thorough study of navigation and wireless telegraphy in order to contribute his utmost to the success of the flight.

The date of the takeoff, September 1, was selected by a French meteorologist, Andre Viaut, who had coordinated his own observations with those of weather stations on the other side of the ocean. It was a misty morning at Le Bourget when the big red-painted plane was rolled from its hangar and the engine started. On the sides of the fuselage were a white question mark and the stork insignia of Costes' wartime outfit, "Escadrille Cigognes," an insignia displayed on other French-flown planes, including the ill-fated Sikorsky S-35 of René Fonck.

Clad in heavy leather flying suits, Costes and Bellonte climbed into the plane's open cockpits, adjusted helmets and goggles and taxied out for their takeoff. Seated in the forward cockpit, which was faired flush with the fuselage and had sliding transparent side flaps, Costes was less exposed to the elements than was Bellonte. Both enjoyed the advantages of considerable special equipment—dual flight controls, a transmitting and receiving radio with a range of about 1,000 miles, food compartments within easy reach, a large tank of drinking water which could be quickly detached, parachutes, inflatable boats, and a kite to keep a wireless aerial aloft.

Only a short time before the takeoff Costes had decided to discard the two overload fuel tanks. He estimated that the main tanks would be sufficient for a 50-hour flight of well over 5,500 miles at a cruise speed of 110 miles an hour. This, he felt, would prove enough to carry them safely to New York, despite headwinds and possible drifting off course. Lightening the load enabled the *Question Mark* to lift off after a run of only 45 seconds, the first transatlantic departure to be made without serious risk of a fiery crash at the outset.

Only a small crowd looked on as the *Question Mark* took off at 10:55 A.M., for this was thought to be just another test flight. But Costes and Bellonte flew due east along the Seine and headed out over the English Channel in clearing weather. Southampton, England, slipped by on their right and, at 2:45 P.M., southern Ireland. They were on course and trouble-free, a situation which prevailed for much of the flight.

The radio functioned perfectly and Bellonte was able to keep in touch with the big ocean liners, *Ile-de-France*, *Berengaria*, and *Bremen*. The headwinds proved no worse than expected and most of their problems came from winds which blew across the course from north to south. But Bellonte's navigation controlled the problem and Costes kept the plane's nose angled northward to offset the drift. At one point they lost almost an hour searching for an opening through dense clouds.

The long night found them keeping a close watch on their fuel consumption, for this remained a factor not to be taken lightly, especially since they had taken off with less than their maximum fuel load. Nearing the North American continent, they found the usual walls of fog, but Costes' years of experience and Bellonte's continued good navigation saw them through. At 6:00 A.M., September 2, they passed their landfall, St. Pierre Island off the southern coast of Newfoundland. The fog began to thin

With fighter plane escort, the Question Mark *crosses Manhattan Island as it nears end of its Paris-New York flight.*

as they flew southward and had become a mere haze when they were sighted over Nova Scotia at about 9:30 A.M.

Excitement grew, both in the United States and France, as reports of the *Question Mark*'s progress were radioed to the world. The sightings over Nova Scotia were followed by word from Old Orchard Beach, Maine, and from Boston. By the time Costes and Bellonte reached New York (after flying through a thunder shower over Long Island) a squadron of fighter planes was aloft to escort them on a triumphal swing over Manhattan and across the East River to Curtiss Field where 25,000 persons had gathered to watch them land.

They touched down at 7:12 P.M. and among the first to greet them was Charles Lindbergh. By the route they had taken they had flown somewhat more than 3,800 miles in 37 hours, 17 minutes at an average speed of about 104 miles an hour. The east-west crossing had taken only 3 hours, 47 minutes more than

Lindbergh's flight, but had consumed two-and-a-half times more fuel and had required, in this case, an engine three times as powerful as the Whirlwind of the *Spirit of St. Louis.*

After a ticker tape parade up Broadway on September 3, Costes and Bellonte flew to Dallas, Texas, the next day in just under 12 hours. There they were greeted by another huge throng and received a $25,000 prize for making the first flight from Paris to Dallas. President Hoover honored them at a luncheon in Washington three days later and, on September 15, Costes and Bellonte left New York in the *Question Mark* for a goodwill tour of the United States, covering 16,387 miles.

Returning by sea to France (along with the *Question Mark*),

Costes and Bellonte at Brainard Field, Hartford, Connecticut, during their tour of the U.S. in 1933. At right, in light suit, is Governor John Trumbull of Connecticut.

UNITED TECHNOLOGIES CORPORATION

The Question Mark *as displayed today in the Paris Air Museum at Le Bourget Field. Foreground: Replicas of Lindbergh's Standard Steel propeller and Wright Whirlwind engine.*

they flew their now-famous plane from the port of Le Havre to Paris on October 24 to the tumultuous applause of their countrymen. Costes was promoted to Commander of the Legion of Honor and Bellonte was made an officer of the same organization. Costes later received the highly prized Gold Medal of the Federation Aeronautique Internationale, sharing this honor with Lindbergh.

Dieudonne Costes and Maurice Bellonte—winners of transatlantic honors for France, completing the quest which had begun so tragically with Nungesser and Coli and the *White Bird* more than three years before.

Left: *The* Bremen *as it looks today at The Henry Ford Museum in Dearborn, Michigan.*

8 THE BIG BOATS OF

GENERAL BALBO
First Mass Crossings _____

IT WAS A SIGHT to behold, the most spectacular in the whole decade of early transatlantic flights. Twenty-five flying boats, huge double-hulled, twin-engined craft, formed up on the waters of Lake Orbetello, Italy, spray streaming out behind them as they sped over the surface in parade precision.

Amid the din of their 50 engines, the big seaplanes lifted from the lake in three-plane units, arrow-shaped, one after another, then climbed north toward the Alps and their first stop, Amsterdam, Holland, 870 miles away.

Led by thirty-seven-year-old General Italo Balbo, the Italian Air Armada (24 planes plus another carrying spare parts) was off on one of the great aerial feats of the decade—a mass flight

At thirty-seven, General Italo Balbo was in Fascist Italy's top command.

across Europe and the North Atlantic to North America, and then on to the Century of Progress International Exposition (Chicago World's Fair), a distance of about 6,100 miles. The project also called for a return transatlantic flight, with a stop at New York.

Ahead of the Armada lay the usual hazards of early transatlantic flights—fog, clouds, storms, and mechanical troubles—all magnified multifold by the sheer size of the endeavor. Balbo's first flight challenge was to lead the formation of flying boats through the towering Alps, following the passes and maintaining an altitude of not less than 12,000 feet.

The liftoff from Lake Orbetello took place on July 1, 1933, but Balbo's mass flight could trace its earliest beginnings back two-and-a-half years to January, 1931. In that month Balbo led a smaller flight of big flying boats across the South Atlantic from Rome to Natal, Brazil, with stops in Spain, Spanish Morocco, and Portuguese Guinea. Fourteen ships took off on that flight, including two with spares, but only 11 made it to Brazil. Two were lost in fatal night crashes before leaving the African continent, while a third was forced down at sea, its crew rescued by one of the several naval vessels posted along the route.

On their final leg the 11 flying boats braved a flight across the unexplored Brazilian jungles, reaching Rio de Janeiro on January 15. There they were delivered to the Brazilian government and the fliers returned home by sea. His first attempt at a mass flight, marred by the loss of three aircraft and the lives of five airmen, led General Balbo to admit that he would sooner fly the ocean three times alone rather than try it again in formation. (The American world fliers of 1924 had learned how difficult it was for even two airplanes to fly together over a long ocean crossing.)

Yet Balbo was generally pleased with the performance of his planes and their engines. Thus, in the summer of 1933, he found himself airborne again, only this time on a far more ambitious flight. A former journalist who had risen quickly to the top command of the new Fascist Party, Balbo insisted on the most painstaking preparations for the 1933 flight. If successful, he knew, it would add much to the prestige of Fascist Italy. (In proof of that point, the "official logbook" of the flight, issued later at the Chicago World's Fair, contained these stirring words in describing the flying boats: "This is the most perfect combination of material: Italian hydroplanes, Italian motors, Italian instruments for navigation, the whole animated by the inflexible will to risk and to succeed, which today constitutes the essence of the new soul of Fascist Italy which, in the glorious tradition of Rome of the Caesars, conquered its place in the world in the name of the Soldier King under the auspices of the Duce.")

Some 300 men, besides the 100 who made up the plane crews, supported the flight. They manned repair bases set up at each stop along the route—Amsterdam; Londonderry, Ireland;

Reykjavik, Iceland; Cartwright, Labrador; Shediac, in the Canadian province of New Brunswick; Montreal; and Chicago. No stop was scheduled for Greenland, but a base was set up at Julianehaab on Greenland's southwest coast in case the always uncertain weather in that area forced a change in plans.

The bases served also as weather and radio outposts, vital services to the Armada, which was to maintain constant communication with New York, Rome, and many radio stations en route. An Italian Air Force yacht, the *Alice*, was sent to Labrador to serve as a floating hotel for the plane crews. Italian and British vessels were spotted along the ocean route and an Italian submarine patrolled the North Atlantic. Nothing, Balbo hoped, was being left to chance.

The planes' crews, specially chosen a year in advance, had undergone months of intensive training, with emphasis on physical fitness. There were four to a plane—commander-pilot, second pilot, radio operator, and engineer-mechanic. The aircraft were Savoia-Marchetti S-55X flying boat-bombers with a basic design dating back ten years. A veteran of many long-distance flights, the S-55X had broken fourteen world records in 1926 for speed, lift, and altitude.

Set beneath the center section of the S-55X's 80-foot wing were two boat hulls, with tapering, V-shapèd booms leading to a triple-ruddered tail section set well clear of the water. The pilots sat back of a windshield in the wing center section, while the other crewmen rode in the twin hulls. Two 800-horsepower Ascotta-Fraschini water-cooled engines, set in tandem, were mounted on struts high above and to the rear of the pilots' cockpit. The engines, each with 18 cylinders, drove two three-bladed propellers, one pulling, the other pushing. The S-55X cruised at 145 miles an hour and had a normal cruising range of 2,250 miles. Its overall design—distinctive, rugged and graceful—made the S-55X an excellent craft for ocean flight and probably the most efficient seaplane of the transatlantic decade.

Balbo took special care with the formation flying procedures

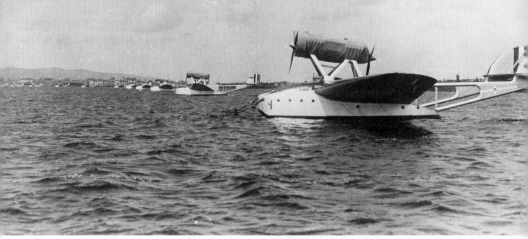

Twelve of General Balbo's 24 Savoia-Marchetti S-55X flying boats at anchor on Lake Orbetello in Italy before the epic mass flight across the North Atlantic.

which had to serve in foul weather as well as fair. The Armada was divided into eight flights of three planes each, two flights bearing black markings, two red, two white, and two green. For quick recognition, the planes bore a system of star and circle markings and were further distinguished by the letter "I" followed by the first four letters of the pilot's name (I-BALB, for example, for Balbo's plane). The Armada's three-plane units flew one behind the other, with the lead plane slightly higher than the one following it. Thus Balbo, looking back, had an instant view of the entire formation which stretched out behind him like the steps of a descending stairway.

After crossing the snowcapped Alps the Armada dropped down and followed the Rhine to the Dutch seaplane base at Schellingwoude on the Zuider Zee, a few miles from Amsterdam. The big flying boats landed, still in formation, and the flight seemed off to a fine start. Suddenly one plane, touching down too heavily, flipped over on its back, injuring three crewmen and drowning the engineer-mechanic, Sergeant Quintavalle. It was a tragic beginning, but there was no time for tears; when the Armada took off for Ireland the next day the spare aircraft had

Above: *Months of flying practice preceded the mass transatlantic flight of the Savoia-Marchetti flying boats.*

Left top: *Twin-hulled S-55X is refueled on Lake Orbetello.*
Left center: *An S-55X in Italy. Note the mounted engine.*
Left bottom: *A Savoia-Marchetti flying boat takes off.*

taken the place of the wrecked machine so that the flight still had 24 planes.

Low clouds over the North Sea forced the formation to fly barely clear of the waves, but over Scotland clear skies prevailed. Later, five British seaplanes escorted the Armada through foggy conditions over the Irish Sea to a safe landing on Lough Foyle, Londonderry, in northern Ireland. Reports of bad weather at Reykjavik delayed departure for Iceland until July 5. The formation finished the 930-mile hop to Reykjavik that evening despite fog which forced the planes down to a height of 100 feet at times.

A stretch of bad weather over Labrador delayed Balbo's take-off from Iceland until July 12. Ahead of the Armada lay the same treacherous 1,500-mile challenge which nine years before had almost ended the round-the-world journey of the Army's

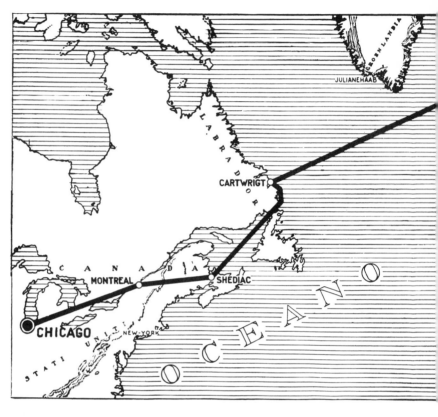

Map showing the route of the mass flight across the Atlantic.

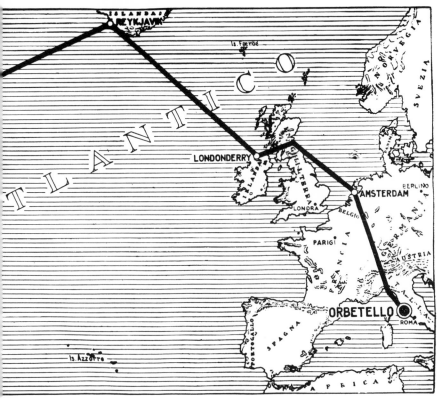

UNITED TECHNOLOGIES CORPORATION

The Armada reached Chicago on July 15, 1933.

PLACES AND DISTANCES

DISTANCES

. . . .	1400 Km.	870 Miles
. . . .	1000 "	630 "
. . . .	1500 "	930 "
. . . .	2400 "	1500 "
. . . .	1200 "	800 "
. . . .	800 "	500 "
. . . .	1400 "	870 "
. . . .	1600 "	1000 "
	11300 Km.	7100 Miles

Chicago and *New Orleans*. Leaving Iceland, Balbo and his men soon met the same icy fogs that had proved such a nightmare to the four Army fliers. The Italians, too, tried to climb above the clouds, but the cold forced them to drop down again to near sea level. The fog got worse and they passed south of Greenland without even seeing its mountainous coastline. It was at this point of greatest danger that their long training as a unit paid off.

With visibility near zero the wireless receivers in each plane sputtered into life as Balbo called the roll, each pilot answering by name. The commander then ordered them to fly in spread formation, to hold strictly to their assigned altitudes and to maintain a propeller speed of 1600 revolutions per minute. The precise following of these orders saw all 24 planes through to a safe touchdown at Cartwright, Labrador, 12 hours after their takeoff from Iceland. This performance, over by far the longest leg of the journey, would have been excellent even in clear weather. It bordered on the miraculous under the blind flying conditions which had plagued the pilots for hours on end.

Balbo and his intrepid airmen were off again the next morning, reaching Shediac after an uneventful flight of 900 miles. The flying boats reached Montreal on July 14, after a four-hour hop from Shediac, as thousands of cheering onlookers lined both banks of the St. Lawrence River. Balbo, the first to land, stared in dismay as a swarm of motorboats sped out from the shore to greet him, many of them directly in the path of planes still in their landing approaches. His shouted warnings contained some choice Italian profanities. A radio announcer, thinking the general was starting his arrival speech, thrust a microphone before him. Thus, the commander's colorful tirade was broadcast to the world—with special effect on those listeners who spoke Italian. There were no accidents, thanks mainly to some alert climbs and turns by the pilots. High overhead a skywriter spelled out a welcome, "Viva Italia."

On the 870-mile final leg to Chicago, Balbo, advised that a storm lay dead ahead on his course, led his planes northward. Despite his planning, though, he found he had no maps of this section of Canada. To add to the confusion, the final flight of three planes had failed to get word of the course change and soon found themselves in the storm. Contrary to predications, however, it gave them no serious trouble.

Meanwhile, Balbo radioed the separated flight to meet the rest of the formation over Detroit where, despite the lack of maps, all 24 planes joined up again. Army pursuit planes from nearby Selfridge Field also joined up and escorted the Armada to a landing on Lake Michigan at Chicago. Huge throngs, double those at Montreal, and including federal, state, and city officials, along with thousands of proud Italian-Americans, welcomed the fliers.

The next morning, already hailed as the stars of the World's Fair, Balbo and his men marched to Chicago's Holy Name Cathedral for a Mass of Thanksgiving for their safe arrival. That night, at a banquet, Balbo solemnly called the roll of his aviators, each man standing up as his name was called—all except Sergeant Quintavalle who had died in the accident at Amsterdam. His name led the list and as Balbo called it out the whole squadron answered as one man.

Balbo's achievement proved to be a triumph (if only a temporary one) for Benito Mussolini's Fascist government, then celebrating its tenth anniversary. More than 100,000 people jammed Chicago's Soldiers' Field to hail the general and his Armada. Illinois celebrated Italo Balbo Day on July 15 and a Chicago street was named in his honor. In New York (which the Armada reached on July 19) there was the traditional ticker tape parade up Broadway, with a tumultuous detour through the city's Little Italy, then the home of a million Americans of Italian ancestry. On July 20 Balbo lunched with President Franklin D. Roosevelt, presented him a gold medal commem-

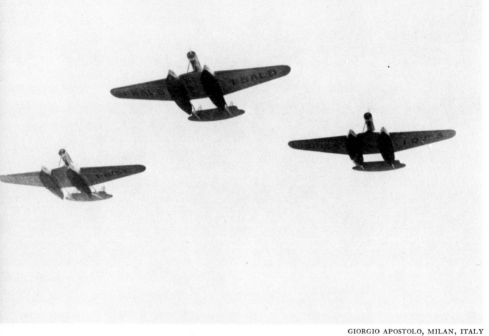

Balbo's plane led this formation over Chicago.

Nearing end of historic mass flight, four of Balbo's planes fly over Lake Michigan and the Chicago World's Fair, July 15, 1933.

The Air Armada at rest on Lake Michigan after arrival at Chicago.

Chicago skyscrapers form a backdrop for one of the 24 twin-engine flying boats of the Armada.

A ticker tape parade up Broadway honored Balbo and his flyers in New York.

orating the flight, and placed a wreath on the Tomb of the Unknown Soldier.

The Armada's voyage home was marred by weather delays, forced landings, another accident, and Balbo's growing worry that something might happen to prevent completion of the flight in triumph. Leaving New York on July 25, the Armada flew low up the northeast coast and out over the sea to Shediac. En route, two planes were forced to land at Portland, Maine, for fuel. The next day, near Shediac, another was forced down with a faulty water pump. These incidents, though minor, combined with a stretch of bad weather to bring a long delay. On July 31, Balbo, fearing the weather along the Great Circle route, especially fog over the Irish coast, decided to return by way of the Azores and Portugal. On August 8 the Armada took off for the Azores where clear skies and the entire population of the island of Fayal greeted the airmen on their arrival. Only a stop at Lisbon, Portugal, stood between the Armada and a triumphal return to Rome.

Balbo's fears were at least partially realized the next morning when one flying boat flipped over during the takeoff run, killing a crewman and injuring three others. The Armada, reduced below its full strength of 24 planes for the first time, flew on to Lisbon and, on August 12, completed the 1,400-mile final leg to Rome. There, Mussolini gave the airmen an unprecedented honor—a march through the Arch of Constantine and along the Imperial Way, a privilege previously reserved only for the victorious legions of ancient Rome.

Balbo and his men, national heroes, received promotions. The general became Italy's first Air Marshal and later governor-general of Libya. In June, 1940, during World War II, an airplane was shot down over Tobruk, North Africa, by an Italian antiaircraft battery when it failed to give a correct identification signal. Aboard was Italo Balbo, his record of careful planning and good luck finally ended at age forty-four.

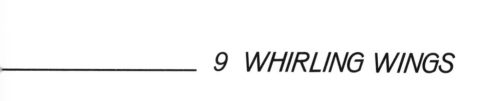

9 WHIRLING WINGS

Across by Copter, Nonstop —————

HELICOPTERS, LIMITED IN speed and range by the very qualities that enable them to hover and to land and take off vertically, stepped out of their class in the 1950s and '60s to challenge the icy North Atlantic. They did so with surprising success and no loss of life, demonstrating their reliability (if not their efficiency for long flights), as well as the skill of the crews who flew them.

Historically, helicopter development has trailed that of fixed-wing airplanes by more than three decades. The Wright brothers first flew their powered aircraft in 1903, while the helicopters of Heinrich Focke and Igor Sikorsky (generally accepted as the first truly successful copters) made their initial hops in 1936 and 1939, respectively.

U.S. AIR FORCE

The first Atlantic crossing by helicopter was made in 1952 by two Air Force S-55s, Hop-A-Long *(shown here) and* Whirl-O-Way. *The flight required six stops.*

That time span of roughly three-and-a-half decades also held true for the first crossing of the Atlantic by rotary-winged aircraft. The NC-4 and the Vimy, as we have seen, flew the Atlantic in 1919. It was not until the summer of 1952 (33 years later) that two U.S. Air Force H-19s (Sikorsky S-55s) made the first helicopter crossing of the Atlantic. The 21-day trip—long, rambling and weather-delayed—required six stops. A C-54 transport plane went along, carrying navigational aides and support equipment. The trip began at Westover AFB, Massachusetts, and ended almost 4,000 miles away at Wiesbaden, Germany. The ocean crossing was made by way of Labrador, southern Greenland, Iceland, and Scotland. The mission, delivery of the two choppers to an air rescue squadron in Germany, testified to the skill and courage of the pilots—Captains Vincent Mc-

Govern, Harry Jeffers, and George Hambrick, and Lieutenant Harold Moore. But it also showed that helicopters, at least at that time, were somewhat out of their element in ocean flying.

In the spring of 1963 the *Otis Falcon*, a U.S. Air Force CH-3B

In 1963, the Otis Falcon *made the second helicopter crossing of the Atlantic. It took seven stops for the 4,337-mile trip from Otis AFB on Cape Cod to Paris.*

SIKORSKY AIRCRAFT

The Otis Falcon *arrives over Paris on June 5, 1963.*
SIKORSKY AIRCRAFT

(Sikorsky S-61A) flew from Otis AFB, Cape Cod, Massachusetts, to the Paris Air Show at Le Bourget Field where it landed
on June 5. The 4,337-mile trip took 10 days and required seven
stops. Fog over southern Greenland forced the *Falcon* to fly to
Baffin Island, far north of its planned route. As a result, when
the *Falcon* resumed its flight eastward it became the first helicopter to cross the Greenland ice cap which rises 11,000 feet
above sea level. Captains John Arthurs, William Lehmann, and
William Scott III took turns at the helicopter's controls.

During 1965 and 1966 three civilian copters (Sikorsky S-
61Ns) crossed the Atlantic on delivery flights to Europe, all over
the Greenland ice cap and all with the usual stops en route. The
pilots were Ross Lennox, United Aircraft of Canada, Ltd.;
Thomas Scheer, Okanagon Helicopters, Ltd., Canada; and Kjell
Bakkeli and Michael Boxill, both of Helikopter Service, Norway.
Lennox flew on all three trips.

Easily the most spectacular, and probably the most significant, of the early transatlantic helicopter flights came in 1967.
This was the dramatic hop of two U.S. Air Force HH-3E (Sikorsky S-61Rs) from New York to Paris. This flight, carefully
planned and brilliantly executed, was the first helicopter nonstop crossing of the Atlantic. The achievement had its beginnings in 1965 and '66 when the Air Force experimented with in-
flight refueling of H-3-type helicopters, rescue aircraft known as
the "Jolly Green Giants." The aim was to greatly increase the
range and effectiveness of the copters on their rescue missions.
On December 29, 1966, an HH-3E stayed aloft for 18 hours,
flying 2,530 miles with four in-flight refuelings from a Lockheed
HC-130P tanker, a four-engined turboprop transport modified
for air refueling of helicopters. The flight proved the concept
was practical and paved the way for the epic transatlantic dash
of the two Jolly Greens six months later.

Toward the end of May, 1967, the HH-3Es were poised at the
U.S. Naval Air Station, Brooklyn, New York, for the long flight

Crews of the two helicopters that made the first nonstop crossing of the Atlantic. Standing, left to right: Major Herber Zehnder, aircraft commander; Major James Hartley, pilot; Captain Clifford J. Buckley, flight surgeon; Captain Gregory Etzel, copilot; Technical Sergeant Harold Schrader, flight engineer. Kneeling, left to right: Major Donald B. Maurras, aircraft commander; Captain Donald Alford, pilot; Captain Charles Dunn, copilot; Staff Sergeant Dennis Palmer and Technical Sergeant Marx Richardson, both flight engineers.

which was to end at Le Bourget Field June 1—"Helicopter Day" at the 27th Paris Air Show. Both the copters and their crews were from the Air Force's 48th Aerospace Rescue and Recovery Squadron based at Eglin AFB, Florida. They were to follow the Great Circle route at first, but then to veer north and pass close to the southern tips of Greenland and Iceland. This was a longer but safer route, for it kept the copters within range of land should they miss an in-flight refueling. Eight air-to-air refuelings were planned, nine if necessary.

The two Jolly Greens lifted off from Brooklyn at 6:05 A.M. May 31, as scheduled, each with a five-man crew aboard. Commanding one chopper was Major Herbert Zehnder, of Baden, Pennsylvania; Major Donald B. Maurras, of Lafayette, Louisiana, had charge of the second ship. Zehnder's crew included Major James Hartley and Captain Gregory Etzel, pilots; Technical Sergeant Harold Schrader, flight engineer, and Captain (Dr.) Clifford Buckley, chief flight surgeon of the Aerospace Rescue and Recovery Service. Flying with Maurras were Captains Donald Alford and Charles Dunn, pilots; Technical Sergeant Marx Richardson and Staff Sergeant Dennis Palmer, both flight engineers.

Crew safety was a major consideration, from the choice of the longer northern route to such procedures as burning fuel first from the copters' external "drop" tanks (in order to fly with them empty as long as possible to assure better stability and flotation should a ditching at sea occur). The crews had the advantage of the latest in aircraft design, flight instruments, and communications equipment. There was ample survival equipment aboard, since the primary mission of all the aircraft involved—fixed-wing as well as helicopter—was rescue work.

Despite such advantages there were risks involved. Each in-flight refueling itself was a delicate maneuver calling for skilled airmanship. The copters nestled close to the C-130, riding in the turbulent wake of the huge tanker as the fuel was pumped aboard. The copters were refueled one at a time at each rendezvous, the total time to complete the job for both ranging from 10 to 15 minutes. As the Jolly Greens whirled northeast along the Great Circle route a couple of questions remained: could the delicate task of midair refueling be carried out if they

High over the ocean a Lockheed HC-130 tanker refuels a Sikorsky HH-3E helicopter.

ran into snow, sleet, or violent turbulence, or could the helicopters and tankers even find each other if the weather closed in?

That the flight entailed real risks was tacitly admitted by the Air Force itself when it decided to release no publicity on the operation until the HH-3Es were safely on the ground at Le Bourget. (At least 16, and possibly 18 separate refuelings would have to be handled, an unprecedented challenge.) But information was "leaked" to a news service and the story was on the air and in the headlines not long after the copters had taken off. As usual, genuine news could not long be hidden.

A tanker which took off with the helicopters from New York provided the first three refuelings. The transfers took place near Presque Isle, Maine; near St. Anthony, Newfoundland; and, the third, well out over the ocean toward Greenland. All were handled at about 5,000 feet altitude.

As they neared the southern tip of Greenland the fliers found the weather "beautiful and clear." The fourth refueling hook-ups occurred 175 miles southeast of Point Christian, Greenland, at about 4,500 feet. There they took on fuel from a second tanker which had taken off from Loring AFB near Bangor, Maine. Shortly afterward the weather turned bad and, as Major Zehnder put it later, "We had to fly about 50 feet off the water to avoid icing while the tanker stayed up above looking for a clear space between the cloud layers."

At that point, in contrast to the earlier, more primitive attempts at transatlantic flight, things were going much as planned—except for unexpected headwinds over the ocean. From the takeoff to well beyond Newfoundland, tailwinds had boosted the copters' ground speed to about 150 miles an hour. But during the long, over-water leg adverse winds reduced that speed to as low as 115 miles an hour.

The two Jolly Greens flew in close formation most of the time, with at least one tanker watching over them at all times. "The tankers cruised about a half mile behind us and 500 feet higher," Major Zehnder said later as he recalled the flight. "Much of the time we flew between cloud layers and maintained the 500-foot separation from the tankers except when the cloud layers got too close together. Sometimes because of clouds and rain we could see only the revolving beacon of the other helicopter. We logged about six hours of instrument flight during the trip."

Also adding to the trip's security was a command HC-130 Hercules which flew high cover, checking the weather ahead and relaying the information to the lower-flying tankers and helicopters. The command plane took off from Goose Bay and stayed with the flight throughout the ocean crossing, finally landing at Mildenhall AFB in England.

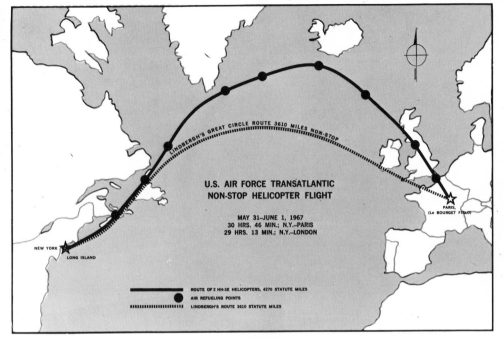

U.S. AIR FORCE TRANSATLANTIC
NON-STOP HELICOPTER FLIGHT

MAY 31–JUNE 1, 1967
30 HRS. 46 MIN.; N.Y.–PARIS
29 HRS. 13 MIN.; N.Y.–LONDON

ROUTE OF 2 HH-3E HELICOPTERS, 4270 STATUTE MILES
AIR REFUELING POINTS
LINDBERGH'S ROUTE 3610 STATUTE MILES

SIKORSKY AIRCRAFT

*Map shows route of the two helicopters from New York to Paris,
compared to the course flown by Lindbergh.*

The fifth refueling took place 200 miles beyond Greenland,
the sixth some 120 miles south of Iceland, and the seventh almost halfway from Iceland to Scotland. All were handled by a
tanker from Keflavik, Iceland, and all were at an altitude of
4,500 feet.

"Refuelings 3, 5, and 7 were the critical ones," Zehnder said.
"In each case we were far out over the open sea with just
enough fuel in our tanks to reach land in an emergency. We took
on from 350 to a high of 920 gallons of fuel per aircraft, with all
hook-ups made from the tanker's left wing tank. There was less
turbulence on that side from the tanker's wing and propellers.
We could have refueled both helicopters at the same time, but
the single hook-up was safer."

Above the Scottish highlands, transatlantic helicopter takes on fuel while the second awaits its turn. This was the eighth refueling.

The eighth refueling was performed over Scotland by a fourth tanker also out of Iceland, the hook-ups being the first over land since the second refueling above Newfoundland. The two Jolly Greens broke formation over England as Major Maurras' ship dropped down to swoop low over London's Heathrow Airport for an official clocking of 27 hours, 14 minutes out of New York, then climbed again to resume its flight for Paris.

The ninth and final refuelings, above the English Channel at 4,500 feet, were carried out only as "insurance" in case of delays getting into Le Bourget Field where Air Show traffic was heavy and closely controlled. Zehnder's copter took a "short drink" from the fourth tanker while Maurras' ship did the same from the command tanker which had taken off from Mildenhall. Without the ocean headwinds the ninth refuelings would have been unnecessary.

Throughout the flight the pilots rotated their duty—four hours on and two off. The rested pilot flew as pilot for two hours, then switched to copilot for two more hours before heading for his bunk aft in the HH-3E's big cabin. The crews later emphasized that the flight was "not just a stunt, but a medical experiment" to determine how well men would stand up under such sustained helicopter operations, especially with the added stress of repeated refuelings. It was a pertinent question, for in Southeast Asia helicopter combat rescue flights were then at their peak.

Dr. Buckley, Major Zehnder, and Major Hartley were wired for continuous recording of heart rates and electrocardiograms. The flight surgeon also evaluated a newly designed electronic blood pressure cuff, intended specifically for use in airplanes, to determine its usefulness aboard a helicopter. All crewmen were closely monitored for medical and psychological signs of fatigue and loss of proficiency. Radio transmissions were taped throughout the flight to obtain further evidences of stress or anxiety.

Dr. Buckley's general conclusion was that 14 to 18 hours would probably be the maximum for long-range operation of helicopters, at least as far as pilot proficiency was concerned. His studies showed that fatigue and reduced crew proficiency became quickly apparent when those limits were exceeded, and would likely be even worse without the incentive of a transatlantic record flight.

Major Zehnder's HH-3E arrived over Le Bourget first, ac-

The first of the two helicopters lands at Le Bourget Field, Paris, on June 1, 1967, after a 4,270-mile flight from New York.

U.S. AIR FORCE

companied by a tanker, the latter with refueling lines trailing from its wings. The two aircraft made a simulated refueling hook-up at 1,500 feet, then quickly separated. ("We were glad to get unhooked after only a few seconds because the air was really rough at that low altitude," Zehnder said later.) The copter landed at 12:51 P.M. Paris time, June 1, for a total flight time of 30 hours, 46 minutes. Maurras' copter touched down a few minutes later. Both flights were recorded as official helicopter speed marks between major cities, New York-London and New York-Paris, with the Federation Aeronautique Internationale (FAI) whose officials had timed the flights.

On the home stretch from Scotland to France tailwinds once more had swept the copters along, the ground speeds reaching as high as 170 miles an hour. In the end, though, the headwinds over the ocean had prevailed: the planned flight time of 27 hours, 48 minutes (to Paris) had slipped by three hours when

Photographers turn from the first helicopter (foreground) as the second copter comes in for its landing at Le Bourget Field.

SIKORSKY AIRCRAFT

At Le Bourget, aviation pioneer Igor Sikorsky poses with crew of the first helicopter to land after nonstop flight from New York.

they landed at Le Bourget Field. The copters averaged 137 miles an hour for the flight, compared with the HH-3E's normal cruise speed of about 150 miles an hour. Their maximum altitude on the trip was 9,000 feet and each copter consumed a total of just over 5,000 gallons of fuel, about 165 gallons an hour. The refuelings were done at speeds of around 130 miles an hour.

The successful flight was the highlight of the Air Show's "Helicopter Day" and, in fact, the top news story of the ten-day show. It had been a dramatic demonstration of the in-flight refueling of helicopters, a concept with one purpose—to extend helicopter range and duration and thereby save lives.

For those who may have thought the flight was easy, Dr. Buckley had this laconic statement:

"Of course," he said, "an unprecedented flight of more than 30 hours over the North Atlantic with icing conditions and difficult weather during refuelings is hardly routine."

Helicopter pioneer Igor Sikorsky, seventy-eight at the time, was among the VIPs who greeted Zehnder, Maurras, and their men at Le Bourget. "I express my deep admiration for this brilliant flight which takes us another step forward in the history of aviation," he told the airmen.

Almost lost in the crowd was a white-haired man for whom the day brought special memories: Claude Ryan, founder of the company that had built Charles Lindbergh's *Spirit of St. Louis* forty years before.

SIKORSKY AIRCRAFT

Claude Ryan, founder of company that built the Spirit of St. Louis, *awaits arrival of nonstop helicopters in Paris.*

Igor Sikorsky greets the commanders of the two transatlantic helicopters, Major Herbert Zehnder, left, and Major Donald Maurras.

10 *THE* DOUBLE EAGLE II

At Long Last, by Balloon _____

WHEN THIS BOOK was begun there remained but one Atlantic "first" unachieved—a crossing by balloon. Before it was finished none remained. Three well-to-do businessmen-adventurers from Albuquerque, New Mexico, relying not on money alone but on research, technology, skill, and experience, plus a fair dash of courage and persistence, had succeeded where seventeen previous attempts over a span of 105 years had failed.

Ben Abruzzo, forty-eight, Maxie Anderson, forty-four, and Larry Newman, thirty, all company presidents, took off on their rendezvous with history at 8:43 P.M. on Friday, August 11, 1978, from Presque Isle, Maine. Their 11-story-high balloon, the *Double Eagle II* (in memory of Lindbergh, the "Lone Eagle"), lifted from Merle Sprague's clover field to the cheers of 5,000 onlookers and drifted slowly away to the northeast, riding a light wind toward New Brunswick, Canada, and the ocean beyond.

One-hundred-and-sixty-thousand cubic feet of helium gas filled the towering, pear-shaped balloon whose upper half was painted silver to reflect sunlight and thus prevent excessive heating and expansion of the gas. Beneath the giant envelope hung a 17-foot red and yellow gondola, twin-hulled to serve as a lifeboat if need be. Dangling under the gondola was Newman's V-shaped red and black hang glider which he planned to fly down when they reached Europe.

Crowded into a shallow 6-by-8½-foot space in the open gondola were sandbags with a total weight of 5,450 pounds and 600 pounds of lead, the all-important ballast needed to control the balloon's altitude. Radios, oxygen masks, sleeping bags, flight instruments, hammers, axes, aluminum lawn chairs, and cameras were among the many other items aboard. Also stowed away, although the flight was expected to take four or five days, was a 20-day supply of food, chiefly coffee, cocoa, fruit juices, doughnuts, raisins, sardines, and a good stock of C-rations.

Based on history, the chances that the *Double Eagle II* would succeed in its attempt to cross the Atlantic seemed slim. Of the many who had sailed away on similar attempts, seven had died, five of them since 1970. Abruzzo and Anderson themselves had failed in September, 1977, when bad weather had forced their *Double Eagle* off course and into the sea off Iceland. Half-frozen and suffering from frostbite, Abruzzo had vowed "never again." But in the warmth of the weeks that followed, he changed his mind. Besides, as his business career showed, he was never one to walk away from a challenge, especially from a job unfinished.

The list of failed flights stretched back to 1873, although balloonists had been dreaming of flying the Atlantic for more than thirty years before. Several balloons were built for the at-

Helium is pumped into the gas envelope of the Double Eagle II *as
the 11-story balloon is prepared for takeoff at Presque Isle, Maine.*

tempt, but all came to grief after only a short hop, without even reaching the Atlantic shoreline. It was not until the middle of the twentieth century that balloonists made any organized and serious attempts to fly the Atlantic.

On December 12, 1958, four Britons—Colin Mudie, his wife Rosemary, Tim Eiloart, and his father, Bushy Eiloart—took off from the Canary Islands in a little 30-foot balloon, the *Small World*. They hoped to ride the trade winds westward to the West Indies or beyond, but ditched after three days aloft. A lot of complex and heavy gear, including a bicycle rig to drive two horizontal propellers for up and down flight (it didn't work), and too many people but not enough ballast aboard had combined to bring them down. Luckily, their gondola proved to be a good boat and they sailed safely westward to Barbados, which they reached January 5.

Sport ballooning gained greatly in popularity during the 1960s, both in the United States and abroad. People again began thinking of an Atlantic crossing. In 1968 Kostur and Winters ditched in their *Maple Leaf* off Halifax, Nova Scotia. On September 20, 1970, the balloon, the *Free Life*, left East Hampton, Long Island, for a transatlantic attempt. Aboard were Rod Anderson, his wife (known as Pamela Brown in her work in TV and the theater), and an English balloonist, Malcolm Brighton. The *Free Life*, unfortunately, was of a hybrid design, complex and heavy, using both helium and hot air. As a result, some balloon experts feared that the flight was doomed to failure from the start. It appeared, also, that Brighton did not give proper consideration to the weather. After flying 500 miles, the *Free Life* went down in a storm off Newfoundland. No trace was ever found of the balloon or its crew.

Balloonist Bob Sparks made two unsuccessful attempts in 1973 and 1975, his first flight in the *Yankee Zephyr* ending in a thunderstorm near St. John's, Newfoundland, and the second in the *Odyssey* 180 miles northeast of Nantucket when his balloon sprang a leak. In both cases Sparks' boat-car proved seaworthy enough to save his life.

On February 18, 1974, Thomas Gatch, a forty-seven-year-old bachelor, lifted off from Harrisburg, Pennsylvania, in a sealed fiber glass cabin suspended beneath a cluster of ten helium-filled balloons each 10 feet in diameter. His plan was to fly at high altitude, probably 35,000 feet, and ride the 80-to-100-mile-an-hour jet stream winds across the ocean, possibly reaching Europe in only two or three days. Gatch carried no ballast, intending merely to cut loose one or two balloons to descend when he reached land. It was not only a risky and largely untested concept, but the equipment apparently was not of the best quality; two of the small balloons burst on takeoff. Gatch, a novice balloonist, was never seen again, although a freighter reported sighting his 190-foot-high rig on February 20, 800 miles southwest of the Azores. In his book, *Bags Up!*, balloon expert Kurt Stehlin theorizes that Gatch suffocated in his sealed cabin from too much carbon dioxide and that another of his small balloons probably burst, dropping him into the sea.

The litany of failures continued. In August, 1974, Bob Berger died when his ruptured balloon, the *Spirit of Man*, plunged into the sea only two miles from his takeoff point, Barnegat Bay, New Jersey. In the summer of 1976 the *Spirit of '76* ditched near Bermuda, with balloonist Thomas being rescued. In January, 1977, the *Eagle*, with Reinhard and Stephenson aboard, ditched southeast of Halifax.

A near success came in October, 1976, when fifty-seven-year-old Ed Yost, a professional balloonist of many years experience, ditched his 80-foot-high helium balloon, the *Silver Fox*, about 230 miles east of the Azores. Yost, a balloon builder and holder of many balloon patents, had prepared thoroughly for the flight, carrying the most sophisticated radio gear ever used in a balloon. Yet he was foiled by the winds, which carried him too far south and would have put him in the westerly trade winds had he not landed. His meandering flight, 2,250 miles in 105 hours, 35 minutes, set balloon records for distance and duration, but still left him short of his goal. A West German freighter hauled Yost's twin-hulled gondola from the sea.

In August, 1978, two British adventurers, Donald Cameron, thirty-seven, and Christopher Davey, thirty-four, came even closer to glory. Beset by storms, unfavorable winds, a rip in their balloon, and their own fatigue, they touched down in the sea only 117 miles and a few hours from Brest, France. They had run out of ballast 3 days, 23 hours, 30 minutes after lifting off from St. John's, Newfoundland, in their $275,000 balloon, the *Zanussi*, named for an Italian appliance company which had sponsored the flight. The aeronauts were rescued by a French fishing boat. They had covered 2,075 miles, but the Atlantic still remained unconquered by a balloon.

It was against that background of failure that the *Double Eagle II* drifted seaward the night of August 11, 1978. In their favor, through, Abruzzo and Anderson had the advantage of their experience and the addition of Newman to share the work load and reduce the fatigue. More important, they had the most thorough and (as it turned out) the most accurate preflight weather analysis ever made for a balloon flight. Bob Rice, chief meteorologist of Weather Services Corporation, a private weather forecasting service, directed the weather watch leading up to the takeoff, looking for exactly the right wind and storm patterns to keep the balloon on a steady course east. He checked his charts to avoid the forces which might carry the balloon too far north (such as the mid-Atlantic storm which had finished the *Double Eagle*'s flight the year before), or too far south (such as the Azores high which had put an end to Ed Yost's attempt).

Rice was one of a flight team based at the balloonists' control center in Bedford, Massachusetts, 15 miles northwest of Boston. There he worked with flight, technical, and communications directors, along with other meteorologists, in tracking the *Dou-*

Double Eagle II *near Newfoundland on its first day aloft. Newman's hang glider, with which he planned to fly down to a landing in Europe, hangs beneath the gondola.*

ble Eagle II, maintaining a close watch of wind patterns, talking by radio relay with the balloonists, and asking airline pilots to keep an eye out for the balloon.

Clear weather and light winds marked the flight's early stages, and the view, in Abruzzo's words, "was magnificent." Newman passed up sleep the first night to marvel at a shower of meteors and the flaming beauty of the northern lights (aurora borealis). A stranger to the art of ballooning, Newman quickly learned that much skill was required to find and use the best altitudes and winds. "There were lots of decisions to be made and often these meant the difference between a successful flight and failure," he said later. "A small mistake at any time could have ended the trip. Once, I felt we were descending too far and too fast, but Ben said, 'No, we will let it go down some more.'" Throughout the flight the line between jettisoning and saving ballast was a fine one, requiring not only experience, but calm and deliberate judgment.

By Saturday morning the *Double Eagle II* had crossed Prince Edward Island and by 1:00 P.M. Sunday was 50 miles east of St. John's, Newfoundland. The control center reported the flight "on schedule and doing very well," but Abruzzo radioed, "We'd like to be farther east than we are." He also reported that they had used 1,400 pounds of their sand and lead ballast which was also "right on schedule." Their plan was to drop enough ballast to rise to 20,000 feet by Wednesday.

When last sighted Sunday evening the *Double Eagle II* was more than 200 miles east of Newfoundland at an altitude of 10,000 feet and sailing due east at 20 miles an hour. By the following evening it was 600 miles northeast of Newfoundland and, in their open gondola, the three aeronauts were beginning to suffer from the cold of the altitude, then about 13,000 feet. Yet, in order to stay with the most favorable winds they knew they would have to climb to higher and colder heights.

The decision to ascend to 21,000 feet or higher was made by

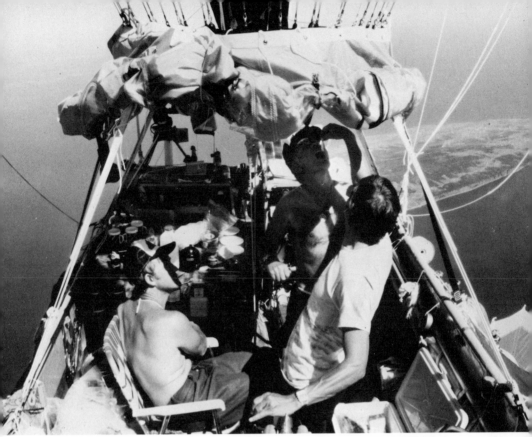

As balloon leaves the coast of Newfoundland, a time-set camera re-cords the scene in the gear-crammed gondola. Abruzzo gets a sardine from Newman while Anderson looks on.

the control center on Tuesday night and radioed to the *Double Eagle II*, even though this meant the balloonists would have to endure temperatures as low as 15 degrees below zero Fahrenheit. For several hours Abruzzo, Anderson, and Newman, working rapidly and with hardly a moment for conversation, carried out the delicate task of dumping the precise amount of ballast to maintain a steady climb. It was not an easy job, for the balloon gained and lost lift as the helium expanded and contracted under the ever-changing conditions of sun and clouds.

By Wednesday afternoon, 120 hours after the takeoff, the *Double Eagle II* floated at about 23,000 feet, drifting east at

Bournemouth, England, slides by 11,000 feet below as Double Eagle II *approaches the English Channel on final day of its historic flight.*

about 16 miles an hour with the coast of Ireland estimated to be dead ahead. Already the flight had beaten Ed Yost's duration record and all looked well. Not long afterward, though, the situation looked anything but well. Cirrus clouds moved in high overhead, blotting out the sun's warming rays. The balloonists found themselves in a condition known as "partial sunset," in which a balloon, suddenly losing its heat and lift, starts a rapid and sometimes dangerous descent.

The *Double Eagle II*, its crew dumping ballast and concerned for the first time during the flight, continued its drop and plunged to the top of a lower cloud deck. In all, the balloon dropped from a height of 23,500 feet down to 4,000 feet. The descent continued and the balloonists had to jettison more ballast. The balloon began to climb again and finally, heated by the afternoon sun, soared to almost 25,000 feet. Skill and experience in ballast handling had paid off; if the crew had panicked and dropped too much ballast the *Double Eagle II* would have risen to even higher altitudes where it would have lost precious helium through its automatic vent. A forced ditching in the ocean short of Ireland would then have been the probable result.

Nearing Ireland, they dropped equipment overboard, chiefly such heavy items as radios, used-up oxygen tanks, and the food cooler. Also jettisoned was Newman's hang glider, which flew around for thirty minutes before dropping out of sight in the clouds below. By ten o'clock that night the *Double Eagle II* was over Ireland, the first of its breed ever to cross the Atlantic. Ironically, the balloonists did not know that they had finally flown into the history books, for the Irish coast lay hidden beneath a layer of clouds. The first word that they had completed the ocean crossing came from a control tower operator at Shannon Airport who radioed the crew, "Congratulations, gentlemen, upon your successful flight."

Abruzzo responded, "Are you sure you're right? We can't see land." Replied the tower man, "My radar has never been wrong." The clouds thinned later and the balloonists saw the lights of Ireland twinkling far below.

As they greeted the sun the next morning the balloonists drifted over the coast of South Wales, sailing along at 11,000 feet. They crossed southern England, reached the French coast at Le Havre (as had Lindbergh 51 years before), flew past Deauville (as also had Lindbergh), and sailed on toward Paris.

Aided by instructions radioed from the control center, the balloonists did their best to find wind currents which would take them not only to Paris but to Le Bourget Field where Lindbergh had landed. But this miracle was not to be, for the *Double Eagle*

Crowds trample a barley field near the village of Miserey, France, cheering the balloonists and tearing souvenirs from the now-deflated Double Eagle II.

II, losing lift and with most of its ballast and gear already thrown overboard, dropped lower and lower over the French countryside, its silvery bulk shining in the evening sun.

By now, sightings and radio reports had alerted the populace below of the balloon's course eastward from the French coast. Thousands watched and hundreds of cars jammed an adjoining highway as the *Double Eagle II* touched down gently in a barley field near the village of Miserey, about 50 miles west of Paris. Cheering crowds, reminiscent of those that surged around the *Spirit of St. Louis* the night of May 21, 1927, charged across the field and tore souvenir fragments from the balloon's collapsing envelope, some even ripping the fabric with their teeth.

Roger and Rachel Coquerel, owners of the field, stood by wondering who was going to pay them for the trampled barley crop. (The balloonists later arranged for payment to the Coquerels.) By the time a French Army helicopter arrived to pick up the balloonists and fly them to Paris a throng of 5,000 milled about the crumpled balloon.

The touchdown had come at 7:49 P.M., Paris time, Thursday, August 17. The *Double Eagle II* had flown 3,105 miles (a record) and had been aloft 5 days, 17 hours, 6 minutes (also a record). The previous balloon records for distance and duration had been held by Ed Yost whose company, ironically, had built the *Double Eagle II*.

In an editorial the *Boston Globe* observed that the flight of the *Double Eagle II* drives home the realization of the lengths to which people today must go to set up new physical challenges for themselves. "People run marathons, climb mountains, and sail round the world," the *Globe* said. "Some pay money to be dropped off in the wilderness with two matches, limited drink-

Be-medalled and happy balloonists received a heroes' welcome in their home town of Albuquerque, New Mexico. Left to right: Maxie Anderson, Ben Abruzzo, and Larry Newman.

DICK KENT

Souvenir of the first crossing of the Atlantic by balloon bears the balloonists' signatures and picture, photograph of the Double Eagle II over the ocean, and the course from the United States to France.

ing water, their wits, and a chance to try their hands at survival. In this sense ours is a world in which we must invent the new worlds to conquer."

With the flight of the *Double Eagle II*, what now remained for the free spirits of aviation to invent and conquer? What is left for those who, as Walter Lippmann put it, "have in them the free and useless energy with which alone men surpass themselves"? Surely there seem no more Atlantic "firsts" left to attempt. Could a sailplane, released at high altitude, make the crossing? Hardly, though someone, "moved by curiosity," may try to find the answer.

What remains for Abruzzo, Anderson, and Newman? How do they top their transatlantic act? Soon after their flight they began dreaming of a balloon voyage around the world, not in the traditional 80 days of Jules Verne, but in 30. Such a trip would require a larger, far more expensive balloon, as well as a flight at higher altitudes. Said Abruzzo at a postflight press conference: "We came an eighth of the way around the world in six days. We traveled over 3,000 miles and therefore my logic is that with a higher altitude and a little more speed 30 days would be entirely acceptable."

In light of their past achievements, who can scoff at this new "invention" of Ben Abruzzo, Maxie Anderson, and Larry Newman, this "new world to conquer"?

Epilogue: HOW PIONEERING

PAID OFF _____

THE MAGIC—AND SOMETIMES tragic—decade of early transatlantic flying is generally accepted as extending from late in
1926 through 1936. During those ten years more than 100 attempts to fly the Atlantic took place, with a toll of 48 lives lost.
Of those attempts, less than half were successful, even though
many were made in stages rather than nonstop. (The totals for
the two decades, 1919–1939, were close to 150 attempts, again
with less than half of them successful, and with 52 lives lost.)

Those pioneering flights, most of which originated either directly or indirectly from Lindbergh's flight, led eventually to the
transatlantic air service we know today. For many years, starting in the mid-1800s, the steamship and the steam locomotive

Boeing 707 initiated transatlantic jetliner operations in 1958.

served as the chief engines of trade and travel. Air transport had its beginnings a little over a half century ago (at the time of Lindbergh's flight) and began to grow. Twenty-five years later, jetliners appeared and brought into being the mass air transport system which now links all parts of the world.

Scheduled transatlantic air service began on May 20, 1939, exactly twelve years from the date on which Lindbergh took off for Paris. On that day a four-engined Boeing 314 flying boat of Pan American Airways left Port Washington, New York, for Lisbon, Portugal, with a cargo of mail. There followed during World War II constant crossings of the Atlantic by planes being ferried to combat duty in Europe, as well as by transports carrying VIPs between the United States and Europe. After the war

four-engined, propeller-driven airliners—notably the Douglas
DC-4, -6, and -7; Lockheed Constellation and Super-Constella-
tion; and the Boeing Stratocruiser—provided transatlantic
service. On October 26, 1958, jetliner service across the Atlantic
was inaugurated when a four-engined Boeing 707, Pan American's *Clipper America*, flew from New York to Paris.

Earlier, several route survey flights had helped pave the way
for the scheduled operations. In July, 1937, a Sikorsky S-42
Clipper, a four-engined flying boat of Pan American Airways,
flew from Port Washington to Foynes, Ireland, with a brief refueling stop at Botwood, Newfoundland. On the same day a
four-engined Short Empire flying boat, the *Caledonia*, of British
Imperial Airways, flew from Foynes to Botwood, later continuing
on to New York. The American craft made the Botwood-Foynes
crossing in 12 hours, 30 minutes, while the *Caledonia*, slowed by
the usual westerly headwinds, required 15 hours, 28 minutes.
The two flights led to a closing of the last gap in round-the-
world air transport, as transpacific routes, established two years
before, had already been linked with connecting routes across
Asia and Europe.

*Huge Boeing 747, widely used in today's transatlantic jet service,
carries well over 300 passengers in air-conditioned comfort.*

BILL OSMUN, FOR AIR TRANSPORT ASSOCIATION

Today the transatlantic route is the busiest in international aviation. Jetliners cross the Atlantic at a rate of one every 15 minutes, carrying more than a million passengers a month at costs considerably less than even the tourist fares on an ocean liner fifty years ago. Today 23 out of every 24 persons traveling between the United States and Europe go by air. They fly in pressurized, air-conditioned comfort in the smooth air of altitudes above 30,000 feet, speeding along at 500 to 600 miles an hour. They complete their flight in six to eight hours (only three or four in the supersonic Concorde), enjoying meals, music, and movies en route—a far cry from Lindbergh's chicken sandwich and 33½-hour ordeal.

Several early aviation experts, were they alive today, would be surprised at such achievements. In 1913, a leading aviation figure, when asked about the chances of flying the Atlantic, saw only a "bare possibility" that a small, one-man plane, with a favoring wind, might get across. "But such an attempt," he continued, "would be the height of folly. When one comes to increase the size of the craft, the possibility rapidly fades away. This is because of the difficulties of carrying sufficient fuel. It will readily be seen, therefore, why the Atlantic flight is out of the question." That "expert" was the surviving Wright brother, Orville.

Others expressed similar pessimism (or lack of vision), especially about passenger travel across the Atlantic. "The simple truth," said one cynic, "is that aerial transportation can never be made to pay."

Another, a noted scientist of the day, scoffed at predictions of "gigantic flying machines speeding across the Atlantic, carrying innumerable passengers" by declaring: "Even if such a machine can get across with one or two passengers, it would be prohibitive to any but the capitalist who could own his own yacht."

Today "gigantic flying machines" speed not only across the Atlantic, but across all the oceans—and they do so not by the hundreds but by the thousands. The latest survey (mid-1978) by the authoritative magazine, *Air World*, showed that the world's 460 airlines (not including the Soviet national airline, Aeroflot) were flying 7,550 turbine-powered aircraft and had 646 more planes on order, for a total of 8,196. Today about half of all air trips are for nonbusiness reasons, chiefly vacations and leisure travel. The so-called "jet set" has now become, in the words of one air transport leader, "the folks next door."

The great strength of modern air transport, which continues to increase, owes a debt to the pioneers, the early ocean fliers, the failures as well as the successes. Anne Morrow Lindbergh, in her talk to a French audience in 1977, reminded them of the words of a famous French flier of a half century before, Antoine de Saint-Exupery, who was also a poet and author.

"Saint-Exupery," she said, "once wrote that in the great creative acts of man, *'Even the gestures that fail'* contribute to the final victory, *'for you cannot divide man.'* "

Today, with the oceans long since conquered, some may view the early ocean flights as overrated or overglamorized. Those who do so might ponder the lesson of Navy Lieutenant Beirne Lay, Jr., who, in 1938, flew an attack plane 2,500 miles from California to Virginia.

Lay confessed that he, like many other fliers, had previously held only a "grudging respect" for the early long-distance pilots, feeling that the acclaim given them was exaggerated and the result of "public ignorance." The aircraft, he thought, deserved most of the credit.

But after his own flight he expressed only admiration for the bravery and endurance of the pioneer long-distance pilots.

"The glamor which surrounds their names may wane in the rising tide of the commonplace which is overtaking all phases of aviation," he said, "but I will never belittle it again."

CHRONOLOGY OF ATLANTIC "FIRSTS"

DATE	"FIRST"	PILOT OR PRINCIPAL FIGURES AND ROUTE	AIRCRAFT
1840	First planned flight across Atlantic	Charles Green of England. Project abandoned.	Balloon
1856	First attempt to fly Atlantic	M. Petin (and 3 others). From Bridgeport, Conn.; Forced down at sea; all rescued.	Balloon *Washington of Bridgeport*
Oct. 15–18, 1910	First attempt with a powered aircraft	Walter Wellman, Melvin Vaniman (and crew of 4). From New Jersey. Ditched at sea; all rescued.	Airship *America*
1914	First airplane crossing planned	J. C. Porte. Project cancelled by start of war.	Curtiss flying boat; 3-engine biplane
April 8, 1919	First east-west attempt	J. C. P. Wood, C. C. Wylie. From England; forced down in Irish Sea; crew rescued.	Short Shamrock; 1-engine biplane
May 16–17, 1919	First flight across	Lt. Cdr. A. C. Read (and crew of 5). Newfoundland to Portugal via Azores.	U.S. Navy/Curtiss flying boat NC-4; 4-engine biplane
June 14–15, 1919	First nonstop crossing	John Alcock. (A. W. Brown, navigator). Newfoundland to Ireland.	Vickers Vimy; 2-engine biplane
July 2–6, 1919	First east-west; first nonstop east-west; first by dirigible	Maj. G. H. Scott (and crew of 30). Scotland to Long Island, New York.	Airship R-34; 5-engine dirigible
July 9–13, 1919	Completion of first round-trip	Maj. G. H. Scott (and crew of 30). New York to England.	Airship R-34
March 30–June 17, 1922	First across, South Atlantic	Sacadura Cabral. (Gago Coutinho, navigator). Portugal-Brazil, with stops. 3 planes used in succession.	Fairey F. III seaplane; 1-engine biplane
Aug. 2–31, 1924	First east-west by airplane	Lts. Lowell Smith, Erik Nelson (and crew of 1 each). England-Labrador via Orkney Islands, Iceland, Greenland	2 Douglas World Cruisers; 1-engine biplanes

Sept. 21, 1926	First fatalities	René Fonck (and crew of 3). New York-Paris (2 crewmen killed on takeoff).	Sikorsky S-35; 3-engine sesquiplane
May 8, 1927	First airplane attempt east-west nonstop	Charles Nungesser. (François Coli, navigator). Paris to ?	Levasseur *White Bird*; 1-engine biplane
May 20–21, 1927	First solo; first nonstop New York to Paris	Charles A. Lindbergh. New York to Paris	*Spirit of St. Louis*; Ryan 1-engine monoplane
June 4–6, 1927	First crossing U.S. to Germany	Clarence Chamberlin. New York-Eisleben, Germany	*Columbia*; Bellanca 1-engine monoplane
Aug. 31, 1927	First woman to attempt crossing	F. F. Minchin. (Princess Lowenstein-Wertheim, passenger). England to ? (3 lost)	*St. Raphael*; Fokker 1-engine monoplane
Oct. 11, 1927	First American woman to attempt crossing	George Haldeman. (Ruth Elder, passenger). From New York. Rescued at sea.	*American Girl*; Stinson Detroiter 1-engine monoplane
Oct. 14, 1927	First nonstop, South Atlantic	Dieudonne Costes. (Joseph LeBrix, navigator). Senegal, Africa, to Brazil	*Nungesser-Coli*; Breguet XIX G. R. 1-engine sesquiplane
Dec. 24, 1927	First American woman lost	Oscar Omdahl. (Mrs. Frances Grayson, passenger). New York to ? (4 lost)	*Dawn*; Sikorsky S-36 amphibian 2-engine sesquiplane
April 12–13, 1928	First nonstop east-west by airplane	Hermann Koehl (and crew of 2). Ireland-Labrador	*Bremen*; Junkers W-33L 1-engine monoplane
June 17–18, 1928	First woman across	Wilmer Stultz. (Amelia Earhart, passenger). Newfoundland to England	*Friendship*; Fokker trimotor seaplane, 3-engine monoplane
Oct. 11–15, 1928	First crossing by postwar German zeppelin	Hugo Eckener (with crew and passengers). Germany to New Jersey.	*Graf Zeppelin*
May 12, 1930	First airmail crossing of South Atlantic	Jean Mermoz. Senegal to Brazil.	*Comte de la Vaulx*; Latecoere 28 seaplane; 1-engine monoplane
Sept. 1–2, 1930	First nonstop Paris-New York	Dieudonne Costes. (Maurice Bellonte, navigator). Le Bourget Field-Curtiss Field	*Question Mark*; Breguet XIX Super T.R., 1-engine sesquiplane
Dec. 17, 1930-Jan. 15, 1931	First mass crossing of South Atlantic	Gen. Italo Balbo (and crews). Italy-Brazil.	11 Savoia-Marchetti S-55A flying boats, 2-engine monoplanes
Nov. 26–27, 1931	First solo across South Atlantic	H. J. L. Hinkler; Brazil to North Africa.	de Havilland Puss Moth; 1-engine monoplane

May 20–21, 1932	First woman to pilot a plane across; first solo by a woman	Amelia Earhart. Newfoundland to Ireland.	Lockheed Vega; 1-engine monoplane
Aug. 18–19, 1932	First solo, east-west	James Mollison. Ireland-New Brunswick, Canada.	*The Heart's Content*; de Havilland Puss Moth; 1-engine monoplane
July 1-Aug. 23, 1933	First mass crossing of North Atlantic	Gen. Italo Balbo (and crews). Italy to Chicago, with stops.	24 Savoia-Marchetti S-55X flying boats, 2-engine monoplanes
Sept. 4–5, 1936	First east-west solo by a woman	Beryl Markham. England to Nova Scotia.	*Messenger*; Percival Vega Gull; 1-engine monoplane
July 4–9, 1937	First commercial survey flight east-west	A. Wilcockson; England to Port Washington, N.Y.	Short S-23C Empire flying boat; *Caledonia*; 4-engine monoplane
July 5–6, 1937	First commercial survey flight, west-east	Harold Gray. Port Washington, N.Y. to Foynes, Ireland.	*Clipper III*; Sikorsky S-42A flying boat; 4-engine monoplane
May 20–21, 1939	First scheduled transatlantic air service	L. LaPorte (and crew). Cargo, mail. New York-England via Azores, Portugal.	*Yankee Clipper*; Boeing 314 flying boat; 4-engine monoplane
June 17–19, 1939	First commercial passenger flight	Culbertson (and crew). New York-England via Azores, Portugal.	*Yankee Clipper*; Boeing 314 flying boat; 4-engine monoplane
July 15-Aug. 4, 1952	First crossing by helicopter	Capts. V. H. McGovern, H. C. Jeffers, G. O. Hambrick; Lt. H. W. Moore. Westover AFB, Mass.-Wiesbaden, Germany via Greenland, Iceland, 6 stops.	2 USAF/Sikorsky H-19s (S-55s); 1 engine, 1 main rotor
Oct. 26, 1958	First scheduled commercial crossing by jetliner	Pan American Airways crew. New York to Paris.	*America*; Boeing 707, 4-engine swept-wing monoplane
May 27-June 5, 1963	First helicopter crossing of Greenland icecap	Capt. J. D. Arthurs. Otis AFB, Mass. to Paris, with stops.	*Otis Falcon*; USAF/Sikorsky CH-3B (S-61A); 2 engines, 1 main rotor
May 14–29, 1965	First commercial helicopter crossing (delivery flight)	Thomas Scheer, Ross Lennox. Montreal to London, with stops.	Sikorsky S-61N; 2 engines, 1 main rotor
May 31-June 1, 1967	First nonstop helicopter crossing	Majs. Herbert Zehnder, Donald Maurras (and crews). New York-Paris.	2 USAF/Sikorsky HH-3Es (S-61Rs); 2 engines, 1 main rotor

Sept. 20, 1970	First balloonists lost in crossing attempt	Malcolm Brighton, Rod Anderson, Mrs. Anderson. New York to 500 miles off Newfoundland.	*Free Life*; helium and hot air balloon
Jan. 21, 1976	First scheduled passenger crossing by supersonic transport (SST); South Atlantic	Capt. Pierre Chanoine. Paris to Rio de Janeiro.	Air France Concorde; 4-engine delta-wing monoplane
May 24, 1976	First scheduled passenger crossing by supersonic transport (SST); North Atlantic	Capts. Norman Todd, Pierre Dudal. London-Washington, D.C.; Paris-Washington, D.C.	2 Concordes of British Airways and Air France
Aug. 11–17, 1978	First crossing by balloon	Ben Abruzzo (Maxie Anderson, Larry Newman, assistants). Presque Isle, Maine, to Miserey, France.	*Double Eagle II*; helium balloon

A SELECTED BIBLIOGRAPHY

Abbott, Patrick. *Airship R-34.* Scribner's, New York, 1973.

Abruzzo, Ben L., with Anderson, Maxie L., and Newman, Larry. " 'Double Eagle II' Has Landed!" *National Geographic*, December, 1978.

Brooks, Peter W. *Historic Airships.* Hugh Evelyn, London, 1973.

Collinson, Clifford, and MacDermott, Capt. F. *Through Atlantic Clouds.* Hutchinson, London, 1934.

Delear, Frank J. "Special Report: First Non-Stop Helicopter Crossing of the Atlantic." *Verti-Flite*, July, 1967.

Goerner, Fred. *The Search for Amelia Earhart.* Doubleday & Co., New York, 1966.

Hamlen, Joseph. *Flight Fever.* Doubleday & Co., New York, 1971.

Heiman, Grover. "Balbo's Italian Armada." *Popular Aviation*, September-October, 1967.

Jablonski, Edward. *Atlantic Fever.* The Macmillan Co., New York, 1972.

Johnston, James. "The NC-4 History Preserved." U.S. Naval Institute Proceedings, May, 1969.

McDonough, Kenneth. *Atlantic Wings.* Model Aeronautical Press, England, 1966.

Montague, Richard. *Oceans, Poles and Airmen.* Random House, New York, 1971.

Payne, Lee. *Lighter Than Air.* A. S. Barnes Co., New York, 1977.

Putnam, George Palmer. *Soaring Wings.* Harcourt, Brace & Co., New York, 1939.

Serling, Robert J. "Wrights to Wide-Bodies: The First 75 Years." Air Transport Association of America, Washington, D.C., 1978.

Stehling, Kurt R. *Bags Up! Great Balloon Adventures.* Playboy Press, Chicago, 1975.

Thomas, Lowell. *The First World Flight*. Houghton Mifflin, Boston, 1924.

Wallace, Graham. *The Flight of Alcock and Brown*. Putnam's, New York, 1955.

Wilbur, Ted. "The Glory of Being First." *True Magazine*, October, 1975.

INDEX

THE AUTHOR

FRANK J. DELEAR, former Public Relations Director of Sikorsky Aircraft Division of United Technologies Corporation, was earlier a newspaperman, working as a sportswriter, reporter, feature writer, and aviation editor.

Born in Boston, Mr. Delear was educated in the public schools of Quincy, Massachusetts, and was graduated from Boston College in 1936 with a B.A. degree. He became interested in aviation as a youngster, working at an airport near his home in Quincy, and was in aviation public relations from 1942 when he joined the former Vought-Sikorsky Division of the then United Aircraft Corporation until his recent retirement.

He is the author of *Igor Sikorsky, His Three Careers in Aviation*, *The New World of Helicopters*, *Helicopters and Airplanes of the U.S. Army*, and many magazine articles on aviation.

Mr. Delear is a member of the Aviation/Space Writers Association. He lives in Centerville on Cape Cod with his wife Marion.